Blue Bell Ice Cream

Blue Bell Ice Cream

A Century at the Little Creamery in Brenham, Texas

1907-2007

Blue Bell Creameries
1101 South Blue Bell Road
Brenham, Texas 77833
www.bluebell.com

Published in partnership with Texas Monthly Custom Publishing

701 Brazos, Suite 1600
Austin, Texas 78701
www.texasmonthly.com

Distributed by Texas A&M University Press

Texas A&M University Press
College Station
www.tamu.edu/upress

John H. Lindsey Building
Lewis Street
4354 TAMU
College Station, Texas 77843-4354
979-845-1436
Orders, toll-free in the U.S.: 800-826-8911
www.tamu.edu/upress
orders@tampress.tamu.edu

Researched and written by Dorothy McLeod MacInerney, Ph.D.
Jacket and book design by Derrit Derouen/Decoder Ring, Austin, Texas
Archival photography provided by Blue Bell Creameries and Brenham Heritage Museum

Library of Congress Control Number: 2006908273

ISBN-13: 978-1-58544-594-3
ISBN-10: 1-58544-594-0

Printed in Singapore
1 2 3 4 5 6 7 8 9 10 07 06 05 04 03

Contents

Foreword

Thanks for allowing us to share some bits of our rich history as
we celebrate our centennial year.

As you will see, there have been challenges and triumphs ever since
Blue Bell began its journey in 1907. We arrive at this milestone as
a result of past and current employees who have dedicated themselves
to making and selling "the best ice cream in the country."

Our special thanks go to E. F. Kruse, Ed. F. Kruse, and Howard W. Kruse
for the leadership they provided in guiding the company for
most of its existence. It is such a privilege to work in a business and
within an industry that has brought so many smiles and pleasures
to consumers throughout the years.

And a sincere word of appreciation goes to Dorothy McLeod MacInerney
for contributing her unending work in putting this story together so that
it might be shared. It's a good story—and it goes on from here.

Paul W. Kruse, CEO and President, Blue Bell Creameries

Artwork from Blue Bell's original butter packaging.

GEORGE BUSH

I would like to take this opportunity to commend the Kruse family and Blue Bell Creameries.

I have great respect and admiration for the entrepreneurial spirit that brought Blue Bell to its unparalleled place of prominence and respect. It is fitting that Blue Bell celebrate its 100th anniversary in 2007.

I often think of the wonders of America; and when I see a successful business built by hard work and entrepreneurial spirit, I am proud to salute it.

G. Bush

Opposite page: President George Bush, the forty-first president of the United States, shares Blue Bell Ice Cream with the creamery's Eugene Supak, vice president of operations, and Howard W. Kruse, CEO and president, in 1996.

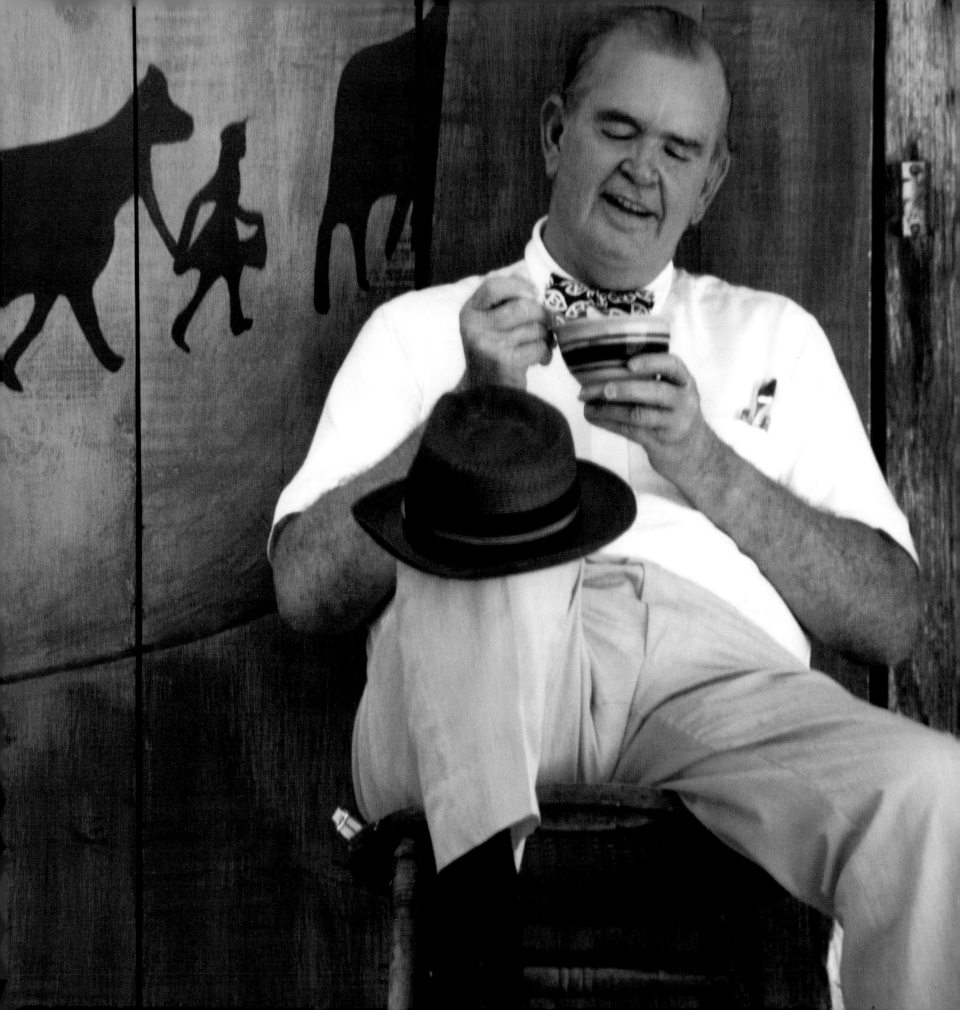

INTRODUCTION

"Ice cream is the happiest food in the world!"

—HOWARD W. KRUSE, BLUE BELL CREAMERIES, BRENHAM, TEXAS

In 2007 Blue Bell Creameries in Brenham, Texas, celebrates 100 years of making people smile. During this century, our ice cream and frozen snacks have generated expressions of delight in many forms.

Wide Grins On February 14, 1996, Mary Lyle and Jeff Oliver of San Antonio, Texas, pledged their marriage vows at Blue Bell Creameries in Brenham. Few people involve us to that extent in their special occasions, but many do serve our products as part of their weddings, anniversaries, birthday parties, and family reunions.

Giggles and Shrieks Another venue where our ice cream excites glee is at slumber parties, with little girls choosing various flavors to concoct smoothies, floats, and banana splits far far into the night. Their squeals of delight are nearly matched at theme parks, where our frozen snacks enhance thrill-filled rides, and at sporting events, where Blue Bell assures triumph no matter the final score.

Closed-Eye Reverie On a quieter level, one taste of Blue Bell's Homemade Vanilla Ice Cream instantly evokes memories of a simpler time of life—porch swings, hide-and-seek games after dark, fireflies, and friendly "Yoo-hoos" at the screen door. Perhaps eating a cherry Bullet or a Fudge Bar mentally triggers the soft jingling of the ice cream truck and the subsequent scurrying to find coins in the sofa cushions or penny jar before the truck moves on down the block.

Soothing Sighs Not only does Blue Bell Ice Cream summon nostalgia for the past, but it also alleviates current discomfort. Cold, delicious ice cream cones of every flavor revive the energy and enjoyment of wilted picnickers and beachcombers on hot summer afternoons. Another group to express "Ahs" upon encountering Blue Bell includes oral surgery patients, who

happily follow doctor's orders as spoonfuls of creamy ice cream provide soothing sustenance. Moreover, our scrumptious products can tempt even the most finicky eaters of the teenage or elderly variety—often to the vast relief of loved ones who are charged with meeting their nutritional needs.

As a matter of fact, the number of ways to enjoy Blue Bell Ice Cream is endless, as is the assortment of delightful reactions to those experiences. We at Blue Bell take great joy and pride in providing pleasure to our customers. However, making delicious ice cream and frozen snacks benefits us as well: Remember, we eat all we can and sell the rest!

You are about to learn that producing and consuming ice cream is not our only bliss. Working with friendly, highly qualified, and dedicated people, creating innovative flavors and frozen snacks, developing meaningful relationships with suppliers, customers, and consumers, expanding into new and varied markets, and meeting the challenges of a highly competitive industry are some of the additional perks to making the happiest food in the world.

This book is a celebration of the can-do spirit of our founders and our employees. It is also the story of a marketplace and a great many innovations. But ultimately it is a tale of people who love their Blue Bell Ice Cream! Our goal in this centennial publication is to convey a shared delight—ours in our work and yours in our products. In the end, we hope you'll wholeheartedly embrace our slogan "Blue Bell is better by a country smile!"

Opposite page: A moment of enjoyment from Blue Bell's 1984 television commercial "Best Tastin' Ice Cream in the Country."

A Blue Bell Time Line

B lue Bell Ice Cream: A Century at the Little Creamery in Brenham, Texas, 1907-2007 records a thorough history of the first 100 years of our company. If you prefer "Blue Bell Light," please sample the highlights of our tale with the following time line. Then relish the photographs and sidebars throughout the book. Once you get a taste of our background, we hope you will devour the rest of the story and discover the people, practices, and processes that have sustained us over the years.

1907

Local investors established the Brenham Creamery Company to make butter, using excess cream from area farmers.

1919

E. F. Kruse became manager.

1936

We purchased our first refrigerated truck and continuous freezer.

1951

Ed. Kruse joined the company full-time and became manager soon after E.F.'s untimely death.

1911

Our first ice cream was made in a wooden tub filled with ice—maximum of two gallons per day.

1930

The company's name was changed to Blue Bell Creameries, after a native Texas wildflower.

1941

Ed. Kruse, age 13, and Howard Kruse, age 11, began working part-time in the plant.

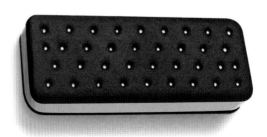

1952

Blue Bell Supreme Ice Cream was first produced and sold in pints and half-gallon containers.

1954

Howard Kruse joined the company full-time and became assistant manager two years later.

1960

John Barnhill joined the company full-time and launched sales in Houston.

The best ice cream in the country.

1969

Howard Kruse developed our number one seller, Homemade Vanilla, and Metzdorf Advertising in Houston began steering our advertising.

1977

A new logo—the Cow and Girl—was introduced.

1958

Blue Bell discontinued making butter to concentrate on ice cream production.

1965

Our first Vitaline machine was installed for automated manufacturing of frozen snacks.

1972

Blue Bell's new package plant was completed, and the original "Little Creamery" concentrated solely on frozen snack production.

1988

Our corporate headquarters and visitors' center were completed.

1989

Blue Bell built a branch in Oklahoma City, Oklahoma, the first site across state lines.

1995

Blue Bell introduced the nation's first complete line of frozen mini-snacks.

1998

Our Web site was established at www.bluebell.com.

2004

Howard Kruse became president emeritus; Ed. Kruse remained chairman of the board; Paul Kruse was named CEO and president.

1993

Howard Kruse took charge of running the company, while Ed. remained chairman of the board. We also opened our third production facility, in Broken Arrow, Oklahoma.

1996

A plant in Sylacauga, Alabama, was purchased and remodeled to serve as Blue Bell's fourth production facility.

2003

Blue Bell introduced lines of southwest flavors and market-specific flavors.

2007

Blue Bell Creameries celebrates 100 years of making people smile.

(1907-1919)

Rocky Road

Rich, dark chocolate ice cream generously sprinkled with chopped, butter-roasted almonds and miniature marshmallows . . .

—From an in-house description of Blue Bell's Rocky Road flavor

Corner Alamo and Douglas St., Brenham, Texas

The 100-year history of Blue Bell Creameries begins as the story of several prominent Brenham businessmen and numerous productive cows. The company founders—an observant lot—noted that the German, Polish, and Czech farmers who cultivated cotton and corn in the fertile, rolling hills also raised happy dairy cows.

Brenham's bovines yielded far more cream than the farmers and their families could consume. With an investment of $2,200 and a goal that the rising tide of cream should float all boats, the town boosters determined to found a company that would be a boon not only to themselves but also to area farmers, townspeople, and businesses. And so it was that in 1907 the Brenham Creamery Company was born of vision, innovation, and copious amounts of cream.

Blue Bell Firsts

Blue Bell was the first plant in Texas to . . .

Manufacture frozen yogurt.

....

Offer unusual-shaped ice cream bars such as the Big Brown Clown and the Mouseketeer Bar.

....

Market 12- and 24-packs of frozen snacks.

....

Price ice cream products according to flavor, allowing the company to maintain quality if the cost of ingredients rose.

....

Pair ice cream and Oreo cookies to create the original cookies 'n cream ice cream flavor.

Blue Bell was the first plant in the nation to . . .

Market a full line of mini-snacks.

....

Sell a half-gallon product made with NutraSweet.

The recipe for success was simple: The Brenham Creamery Company placed its stations for collecting, evaluating, and weighing the cream in town. The farmers, who sold cream in the morning and received their proceeds in the afternoon of that same day, felt flush enough to purchase staples such as flour, salt, and sugar from local merchants during their trips to town. Thus the steady source of income from butterfat sales kept the economic wheels turning for all parties until the farmers could invest the profits from their fall harvests in major purchases.

For its part, the Brenham Creamery Company churned the cream into butter for sale to the townspeople. Early in its history the creamery produced only sour cream butter, as farmers tended to store the cream for up to a week before bringing it to town to sell. Proceeds from the creamery's sale of sour cream butter were nonetheless sweet and generated enough profits to buy additional cream from the farmers, improve the company's butter-making process, and pay dividends to the company's stockholders. The founders' dreams of goodwill and profitability for all were well on the way to becoming reality.

Despite the sound investment logic, solid business experience, and all-around enthusiasm of its founders, the Brenham Creamery Company's path to success proved rocky in the early years, as evidenced by the fact that between 1907 and 1919 the board of directors hired four managers in fairly quick succession.

Faltering Steps

On July 18, 1907, the *Brenham Banner-Press* announced the first of these new hires: "Mr. F. Jensen, late of Alvin, has moved his family to Brenham and will take charge of the proposed new creamery." Newspaper ads later placed by the company seem to emphasize the obscurity of the new man by identifying the manager of the Brenham Creamery Company only as "F. Jansen" [*sic*]. His first name has been forgotten (it may have been Flaor), perhaps because the records show he did little more during his tenure than join the Texas Creamers Association at the company's expense, prepare a circular of instructions for patrons, and install a telephone in the company office. He resigned after the board of directors

Hand-Crank Freezer

Blue Bell's first ice cream was made in hand-crank freezers. The mixture of milk, eggs, and sugar was poured into the inner metal can. A dasher was inserted and attached to the crank through a hole in the lid of the can. Ice and salt were placed in the outer wooden bucket to surround the inner container. As someone turned the crank, frozen ice cream accumulated on the wall of the metal can. The dasher continuously scraped the wall and incorporated more and more ice cream and air into the mixture. After a while, the entire mixture was frozen and could be served.

Early Brenham

Opposite page: The corner of Alamo and Douglas streets in Brenham, Texas, in the early 1900s.

rejected an arrangement he'd made with a Houston concern to purchase the Brenham Creamery Company.

A Steadier Path

On August 26, 1908, the creamery's board elected H. C. Hodde to fill the managerial vacancy. Hodde began his tenure by actively taking a hand in keeping the company afloat: He cosigned a $500 loan with the president of the company, L. A. Niebuhr. Hodde's early performance obviously pleased the directors of the creamery—in less than a year they doubled his salary, from $30 to $60 a month.

One Pound Net Weight
BUTTER
PACKED BY
Blue Bell Creameries
**BRENHAM & GIDDINGS
TEXAS**

Butter Wrapper

Although the Brenham Creamery Company began making butter in 1907, the only existing wrappers are post-1930, when the company's name changed to Blue Bell Creameries and production occurred in both Brenham and Giddings.

Early Production

Opposite page: E. F. Kruse (far right) is seen with employees in the plant in the early 1920s.

Brenham Creamery Building

Following page: The "Little Creamery in Brenham" served the company as its only production facility from 1909 to 1972.

Early in Hodde's tenure the creamery moved from its original location at First and Church streets in Brenham to the abandoned American Cotton Gin building on what is now Chappell Hill Street. Converted to a creamery, this building—with many expansions and improvements along the way—became the company's only plant until 1972. As the official "Little Creamery in Brenham," this facility continues to produce frozen snacks for Blue Bell Creameries today. The Brenham Creamery Company sold its original Church Street location in 1914.

During Hodde's eight years as manager, the Brenham Creamery Company produced more than a million pounds of Clover Leaf butter and expanded sales to Houston, San Antonio, and other Texas cities.

An Ingenious Idea

More significant to the company's future was Hodde's decision in 1911 to make ice cream for the first time. Initially, the creamery produced only two hard-won gallons per day. The butter maker at the company laboriously hand-cranked a mixture of cream, sugar, and flavorings in a metal can surrounded by cracked ice and salt and set inside a wooden tub. Company personnel in a horse-drawn buggy delivered the ice cream that resulted from this age-old freezing process, in its can and wooden tub, to local residents—usually large families who could gleefully consume the ice cream before it melted.

The delight must have been contagious, because at a board meeting on November 11, 1911, the Brenham Creamery Company determined to invest more extensively in the production of ice cream. The board of directors met with J. N. Gruhl, a representative and engineer of the Creamery Package

Manufacturing Company of Chicago, Illinois, and hired his company "to install an ice cream plant and machinery according to a specific contract for $3,380."

The directors also approved H. C. Hodde's purchase of ice cream cans, tubs, a freezer, and an ice cracker for $530.80. The investment proved profitable. During the 1912–1913 fiscal year the creamery sold more than 6,000 gallons of ice cream. The ice cream sales, combined with the butter sales, earned a profit of almost $7,900 for that year—ice cream production had given the company a new definition for the term "frozen assets."

Innovative Equipment

Company insiders were not the only ones impressed with what was going on at the creamery. The plant exhibited such state-of-the-art equipment and processes that in 1912 it drew a visit from one J. L. Thomas, a professor in College Station, and a group of teachers. After a tour of the facility, Hodde served the visitors four flavors of ice cream and invited volunteers to enter the cold-storage room, where the temperature hovered near freezing. Those who braved the cold emerged shivering. This tour, one of the first of thousands of such excursions to the creamery over the next century, solidified the early association of the Brenham plant with the educational facilities in College Station, Texas.

Broader Concerns

Around this time, Hodde followed Jensen's lead in joining the state creamers association and attending meetings of that organization. Soon the company's active interest in dairy issues expanded to the national level, and in 1913 the Brenham Creamery directors passed a resolution opposing a bill in Congress that would allow the coloring of "oleomargarine in

The Batch Method

In the batch method of producing ice cream, the ice cream maker poured ten gallons of mix into the top of the machine. The mix then flowed down into the freezer barrel, where paddles whipped the freezing cream until it reached the desired consistency. This process produced twenty gallons of ice cream because whipping added air and increased the volume. The next step was to fill ice cream packs and deliver them to the customers, mainly drugstores and confectioneries, where townspeople could enjoy dishes of the delicious treat.

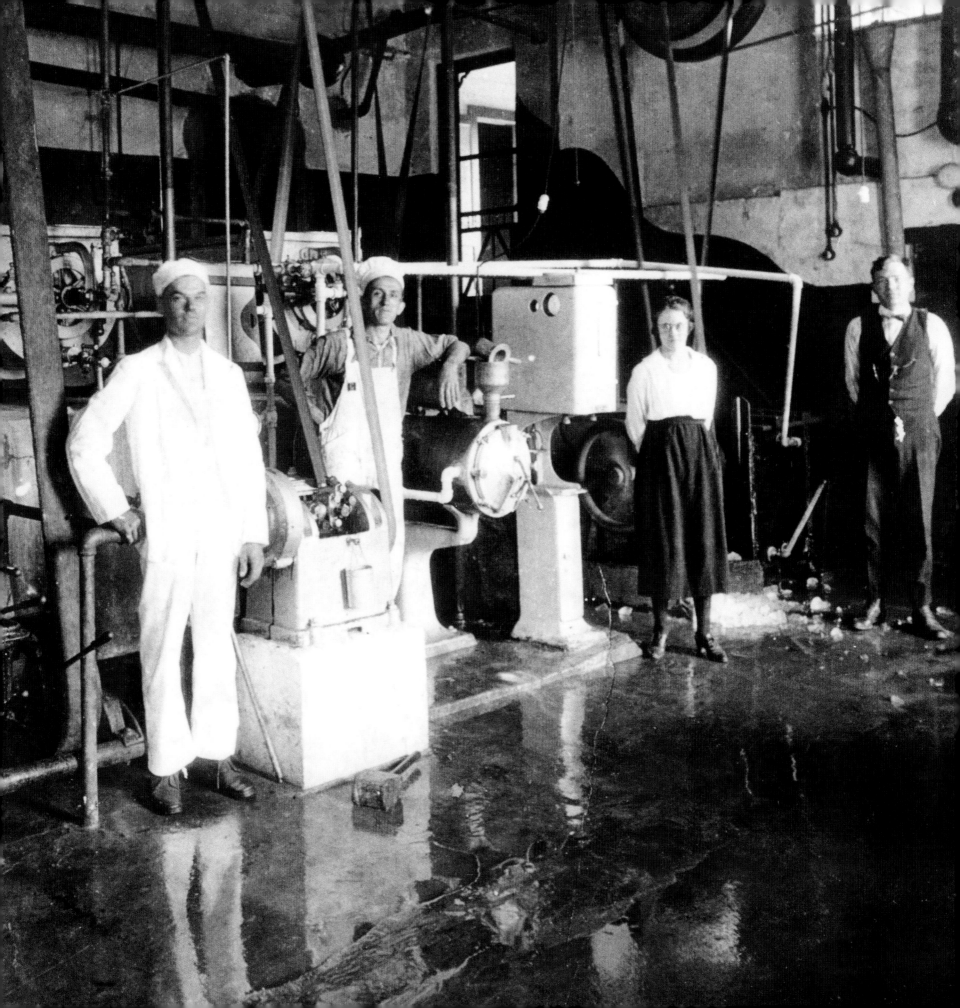

imitation of butter." The company had no argument with uncolored oleomargarine but feared that yellow-tinted oleomargarine would hobble the butter industry in Texas.

H. C. Hodde's contributions to the Brenham Creamery Company were valuable ones and reflected the company's motto at the time: "As good as the best, if not better." Despite his fine work, in April 1916 the board asked Hodde to resign, apparently because of his age. He agreed to remain in his position until June so that he could train the new manager, J. A. Heineke—and make one last innovative deal. He was to arrange for Mr. Druckhammer, a creamery employee, to use his own horse to peddle ice cream on commission. The creamery would purchase the wagon and pay him an increased salary for the extra duties.

Ups and Downs

J. A. Heineke assumed his new position with bravado. The company established cream stations in Carmine in 1916 and Navasota in 1917—and even considered buying a truck to gather cream from the various locations. But while his early tenure appeared promising, Heineke ultimately witnessed a downturn in the Brenham Creamery Company's good fortune. Finances were shaky enough by 1917 that Mr. H. F. Hohlt, a board member and the company's major stockholder, felt obliged to loan the business $2,000. Whether the entry of the United States into World War I caused some of the cash-flow problems is unknown. Board meeting minutes from that year reported the need to reduce expenses and a decision to discontinue the ammonia system for hardening ice cream in favor of "slush boxes." Tightening belts still further, the directors decided that plant employee B. H. Johnson would labor alone except for a single part-time helper during the busy season.

Midway through 1918 the Brenham Creamery Company rebounded a bit. In June the board authorized Heineke to buy another ice cream freezer to help meet the demand for the product. Furthermore, in August the directors voted to pay a drayman in each town to which the creamery shipped ice cream. The men would collect the empty ice cream packers and cans in their carts and deliver them daily to the express train in order to relieve the constant shortage of containers at the creamery.

Wildflowers, Brenham and the surrounding area. Laurence Parent

The End of the Beginning

But all was not smooth sailing. In September 1918 a disgruntled employee's demands precipitated a watershed moment in the Brenham Creamery Company's history. B. H. Johnson, the butter and ice cream maker for the creamery, apparently feeling overworked and underpaid, sent salary and hour demands in a letter to his employer. When the board refused to meet all his terms, he resigned. Although a replacement was quickly hired, the over-all situation looked bleak. The board was questioning Heineke's managerial skills, and Hohlt's loan was coming due. In early 1919 the stockholders seriously considered dissolving the company. Instead, they authorized extended loan payments to Hohlt at a higher interest rate and charged the board with finding another manager for the company. It was decided that Hohlt should contact E. F. Kruse at Camp Beauregard in Alexandria, Louisiana, where he was completing his World War I service. In an act that influenced the company's future more than any other to date, Hohlt asked the twenty-three-year-old graduate of Southwest Texas State Normal College in San Marcos to move to Brenham to manage the creamery.

A Smooth Road Ahead

Things might have turned out differently. At almost the same time, the reputable and intelligent Kruse received an offer from the nearby Burton, Texas, school district to become superintendent, a position that seemed a more natural fit, given his training as a teacher. Nevertheless, he decided to accept the Brenham Creamery offer. Maybe he appreciated the unique challenges he would face in Brenham or perhaps he calculated the opportunity to earn more money in the business sector. Possibly he thought that making ice cream would be exciting. In any case, E. F. Kruse's acceptance of the position of manager at the Brenham Creamery Company in April 1919 set the company on a steady path of growth.

WHEREAS, the Brenham Creamery Company has been operated for some time past without any returns or dividends to the stockholders; and,

WHEREAS, it is believed that the lack of proper management and attention to the affairs of the business are reasonable for this condition; and,

WHEREAS, E. F. Kruse is a man of good business ability, honest, reliable and attentive to business and has signified his willingness to take the management of said business; therefore,

BE IT RESOLVED, by the Board of Directors of the Brenham Creamery Company, that the President of said Board be and he is hereby authorized to employ Mr. Kruse as Manager of the Brenham Creamery Company at a monthly salary of $ 75.00 , his services to begin as such Manager not later than April the 1st, A.D. 1919.

Resolution Hiring E. F. Kruse

On April 1, 1919, the Brenham Creamery Company hired E. F. Kruse as manager at a monthly salary of $75.

Ice Cream Scoop

At left: The scoop shown here dates from the 1940s.

Texas Bluebonnets

Opposite page: The Texas state flower thrives in Brenham and the rest of Washington County during several weeks each spring.

Strawberry

Smooth, creamy strawberry ice cream made with succulent strawberries . . .
—From an in-house description of Blue Bell's Strawberry flavor

EF. Kruse did not turn the creamery around immediately, and it is only by some luck that he was given the opportunity to turn it around at all. He had scarcely begun managing the Brenham Creamery Company when once again the board met in special session to consider dissolving the poorly performing company.

However, Kruse and Hohlt, the newly elected president of the board, successfully conveyed their optimism to the others, and for the second time in its history the Little Creamery felt the swoosh but not the bite of the axe as the company tottered forward.

Confidence Building

Nevertheless, Kruse took no chances. He refused to cash his paychecks for several months until the company's bottom line could withstand the deductions without going in the red. He worked from 7:30 a.m. until 6:00 p.m. six days a week and two hours on Sunday mornings before attending church services. A determined man, he held to this schedule throughout his career at the creamery.

Not only was E.F.'s work ethic evident from the start, but his organizational skills also introduced positive changes at the creamery. He aligned the company's fiscal year with the calendar year and took meticulous minutes at board meetings. More important, with the support of the rest of the board of directors, he judiciously began an ongoing cycle of increasing the customer base and expanding the plant. Early on, he established a cream station in Rockdale, Texas, a decision that continued the tradition of former managers, who had enlarged the creamery's territory for purchasing butterfat.

Soon the directors authorized E.F.'s plan to build an annex to the creamery for receiving and storing supplies. They also approved the purchase of an additional ice cream batch mixer and cooler—at the best possible price, of course. And to replace the company horse that delivered its products,

the creamery bought a motorized (but unrefrigerated) Model T Ford in 1919.

Early Advertising

Another of E. F. Kruse's first endeavors involved stepping up public relations. Within two weeks of assuming the position of manager, he sent free ice cream to the *Brenham Banner-Press*. He also solicited the newspaper's involvement in a contest to name the creamery's brand of ice cream. Until that time company letterheads merely referred to the product as "Purity Ice Cream." On April 11, 1919, the *Brenham Banner-Press* reported that the Brenham Creamery Company would award $10 to the person who suggested the most suitable name "for the superior ice cream now being manufactured." Twelve days later the newspaper announced the winner to be R. W. Buehrer. Of 230 entries, his submission, "Delicious Ice Cream," generated the best response from the judges. In that early stage of his management E. F. Kruse had already elicited favorable public opinion for his products.

Problem Solving

That's not to say everything initially went smoothly for him. Board minutes report firings and hirings of ice cream and butter makers as employees adjusted to Mr. Kruse's professional approach to running the creamery. To further hamper operations, a small fire occurred at the plant in early 1920. Repairs were quickly completed, and a grateful board sent a donation to the Brenham Fire Department and a gift of ice cream to the South Texas Cotton Mills in appreciation for their aid in extinguishing the fire.

Topics of varied wattage charged other directors' meetings. The greatest buzz came from frequent offers made to the board by larger concerns to purchase the Brenham Creamery Company. These were sometimes local offers, but more often queries came from larger companies based in Houston, seventy miles to the southeast. The directors declined to accept the proposals. Occasionally, however, E.F. and the other directors discussed possible sidelines to their butter and ice cream business. At one point they entertained the notion of

Early Ad

The Brenham Creamery Company purchased advertising space in the 1925 Brenham telephone directory.

Milk Can

At left: During the early years of the creamery, metal cans stored milk until it was used in an ice cream mix.

Ladylike Licks

Opposite page: After the 1904 World's Fair in St. Louis, Missouri, Americans used waffle cones as a portable, litter-free, and delicious way to enjoy their ice cream.

Worth the Wait

Following page: In his 1990 painting, artist George Hallmark depicted the anticipated delivery of Blue Bell Ice Cream to the Savitall Market in Brenham.

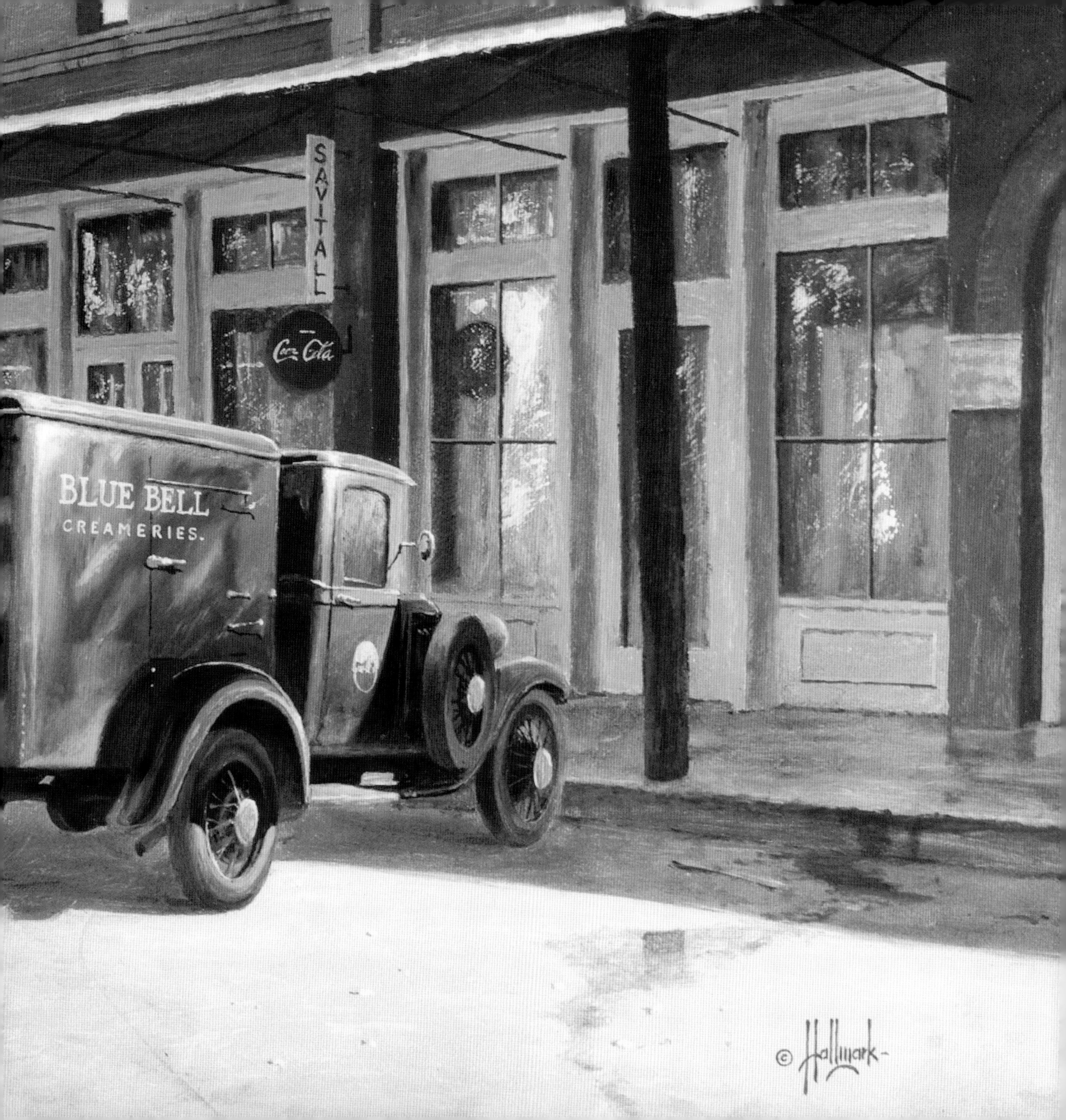
SAVITALL
Coca-Cola
BLUE BELL
CREAMERIES.
© Hallmark

making and selling candy, but they took no steps in that direction. In the meantime, the creamery continued improving the plant, purchasing butterfat from area farmers to produce quality butter, and making "Delicious Ice Cream" in vanilla, chocolate, strawberry, and buttered pecan flavors.

Positive Decisions

For his part, E. F. Kruse remained active in statewide creamery organizations and joined the Rotary Club in Brenham to help address community needs. He also sent a worker to attend short courses at "A. M. College" (today Texas A&M University is internationally recognized for its dairy science program) under the delightfully named Professor Clutter. Like all other key management decisions, proper training of staff was implemented early in the company's history.

In 1927 the Brenham Creamery Company celebrated its twentieth year in business and renewed its charter with the State of Texas for another thirty years. This optimistic step was saluted by the application of plaster to the entire exterior of the creamery building and the painting of a sign on the plant. With the blessings of the board, E.F. also purchased a truck for the company.

Having navigated the many curves and bumps of its early path, the Brenham Creamery was now prepared to pave a smooth road into the future. And so was E. F. Kruse. Over the years, he wisely began investing his personal money in the company, and eventually he became its second-largest stockholder. He set the course for future employees to purchase shares in the company. This policy reflected a core belief in the interdependence of success and employee involvement.

Face-lift

White plaster provided a fresh, updated look for the Brenham Creamery Company in the late 1920s.

Washington County, Texas

Opposite page: Richard Reynolds captures the essence of Blue Bell country with this photograph of cows grazing in a pasture sprinkled with bluebonnets.

Ice Cream Float

Following page: In 1925, the Brenham Creamery Company contributed a festive float for the annual Maifest Parade. A celebration of spring, Maifest has been enjoyed in Brenham since the 1870s.

Spic-and-Span

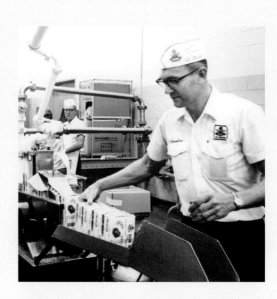

Blue Bell takes pride in the company's long-standing emphasis on clean, sanitary facilities. Even as early as 1912, the *Brenham Banner-Press* reported favorably on the cleanliness of the Brenham Creamery's ice cream and butter production areas.

Cleanliness continues to rule in all plants. Each afternoon Blue Bell employees break down the plant equipment completely and clean each piece thoroughly. The procedure involves rinsing each part in very hot water supplied directly from boilers at Blue Bell. Then a cleaning solution is used to scrub each piece. A thorough rinsing follows. Finally, the equipment is sanitized. This process takes several hours.

Before production begins the next morning, the equipment is thoroughly rinsed and sanitized again. Visitors to the plant recognize the sanitary conditions. A physician from Seguin visited the creamery and wrote on January 31, 2003, "We have had the good fortune to have visited your Ice Cream Factory and were impressed with the entire process. The plant appeared spotless, I truly believe it could be compared to an ideal surgery room set up—in fact, it may be more 'germ free.'"

In addition to the high standards of sanitation, Blue Bell is proud of the fact that its production employees work on a dry floor. Many steps have been taken over the years to provide this safer and more pleasing working environment.

Pictured above: Kervin Finke

Grazing cows, Washington County, Richard Reynolds

MAI-FEST
1925

BB
ICE CREAM
BRENHAM CREAMERY CO.

E. F. Kruse

Eddie Fritz "E.F." Kruse was born in 1895 and reared in Prairie Hill, Texas. He was the youngest of the nine children of Wilhelmina (Lippe) and August Kruse, a successful Washington County farmer. E.F. first attended Blinn College in Brenham and then graduated from Southwest Texas State Normal College in San Marcos. He taught school briefly before joining the U.S. Army during World War I.

In 1919 E.F. became the fourth manager of the Brenham Creamery Company, which he renamed Blue Bell Creameries in 1930. His successful tenure at Blue Bell lasted until his untimely death on October 21, 1951, following major cancer surgery.

E.F. became a prominent figure in the ice cream industry in Texas and served as president of the Texas Ice Cream Manufacturers Association and as a director of the Dairy Products Institute of Texas. In 1981 he was posthumously inducted into the Dairy Products Institute Hall of Fame.

An industrious community leader, he served as a Brenham city commissioner and mayor pro tem, presided over the Washington County Board of Education, and acted as vice president of the First National Bank of Brenham.

He was also president of the Brenham Chamber of Commerce, a director of the East Texas Chamber of Commerce, and a Rotarian. Additionally, he served as a commander of the American Legion and helped organize and command the Buddy Wright American Legion Post in Brenham. During World War II, he was chairman of the Washington County Draft Board.

Active in church work, he served as president of the Brenham Area Lutheran Brotherhood and taught Sunday school at St. Paul's Lutheran Church.

E. F. Kruse married Bertha Quebe on January 22, 1920. The couple had five children: Bertha (deceased), Mildred, Ed., Howard, and Evelyn Ann.

Krunch Bar

Smooth vanilla ice cream on a stick, covered in milk chocolate and crisped rice . . .
—From an in-house description of Blue Bell's Krunch Bar

Despite the stock market crash in 1929, the Brenham Creamery Company began the decade of the 1930s with a spring in its step. Taking a bold leap, E. F. Kruse suggested changing the name of the company to the Blue Bell Creamery.

The name evoked his love for the lavender wildflowers that flourished during the hottest part of the summer—the height of ice cream season—in his hometown of Prairie Hill, just north of Brenham.

Bluebells are not to be confused with Texas bluebonnets, which also appear profusely in the Brenham area but during cool, wet springs. To E.F., the bluebells represented a beauty,

purity, and freshness that he wished to have identified with his products. And, all poetry aside, he may have been inspired to compete with the flowery names of two Houston concerns, the Carnation Creamery and the Lilly Dairy.

New Name

Certainly E.F. was aware of all his competitors' activities, whatever their company names. Blue Bell Creamery quickly became Blue Bell Creameries when the company bought the Giddings Creamery, about thirty miles to the west, in late January 1930 for $8,000. The Giddings branch would manufacture Blue Bell butter and distribute Blue Bell Ice Cream, both of which would also continue to be produced in Brenham. H. C. Wiese managed the Giddings branch until Blue Bell closed it in 1956.

In early 1931 H. F. Hohlt resigned as president and member of the Blue Bell Creameries board because of ill health. The stockholders immediately elected his son, Herbert C. Hohlt, to the board, and the directors chose him as president of the company. Other officers of Blue Bell Creameries at this time included E. F. Kruse as manager, secretary, and treasurer and F. C. Winkelmann, who was vice president. Will Kolwes and T. A. Low also served as directors of the company.

Fresh Product

As the leadership evolved, so did the product line. In response to customer requests, Blue Bell added a new commodity in 1931: sweet cream butter. The *Brenham Banner-Press* made the long-awaited announcement concerning Blue Bell's Supreme Sweet Cream Butter: "The finest product churned from sweet pasteurized cream, which is picked up daily on the sweet cream truck route that was recently established in Washington County, and is said to be far superior to ordinary butter, made from sour cream.... Brenham stores will handle the new product, and the butter will also be shipped to various points."

Additional Problems

Despite all the good news and innovations at the creamery in the early thirties, the wave of the Great Depression eventually rolled into Brenham. The first change was small: E.F. discontinued an ad in the telephone directory. Then the squeeze in profits pressured the board to suspend dividends and reduce wages. Ultimately the company cut the prices it paid for butterfat. To Blue Bell's credit, however, no employee lost his job during the Depression. In fact, in its 100-year

Andy's Assignments

Elton B. "Andy" Anderson (pictured above at left) spent fifty-three years at Blue Bell. Joining the company in 1930 as a teenager, he earned seven cents an hour. He picked stems off strawberries, cut ninety-pound boxes of butter into one-pound blocks and wrapped them individually, retrieved cans of sour cream from the various cream stations in town, chopped wood for the boilers that produced hot water for cleaning equipment, and performed any other task E. F. Kruse asked him to do. Andy was one of seven employees at the time.

After a year and a half at Blue Bell, Andy began delivering butter and ice cream to various locations within the city. He used a car at first and, shortly thereafter, a small truck refrigerated by dry ice.

E. F. and Bertha Kruse

The Kruses pose for a photo during a rare snowfall in Brenham in 1936.

Bluebells in Bloom

Opposite page: E. F. Kruse changed the name of the Brenham Creamery Company to Blue Bell Creameries in 1930. He wanted to reflect the purity and freshness of his favorite wildflower.

First Refrigerated Truck

Following page: Purchased in 1936, the Chevrolet truck could deliver 20 five-gallon cans of ice cream on one route.

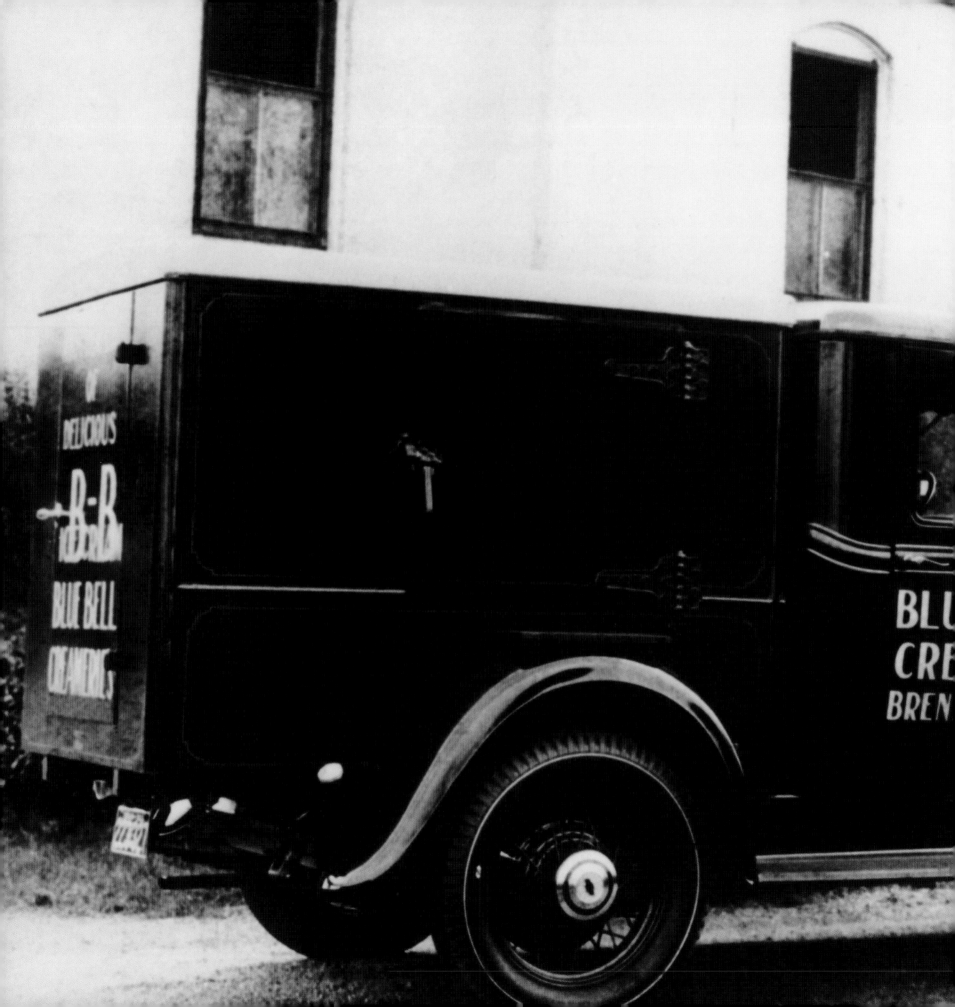

The Kruse Children

Bertha and Mildred stand behind their younger siblings at their home on West Fourth Street in Brenham in 1936. Howard, Evelyn Ann, and Ed. are in the foreground (left to right).

Double-Dip Cone

At right: During the Great Depression, Americans had very little money for luxuries, but many could treat themselves to a nickel double-dip cone once a week. Central Texans could buy their Blue Bell Ice Cream cones at the company's Lotta Cream stores.

Hand-Packed Carton

Opposite page: In 1939 Blue Bell supplied drugstores and soda fountains with pint cartons so that consumers could take ice cream home.

history, the company has never found it necessary to lay off or downsize its workforce. The story of Blue Bell is ultimately the story of the people who built and maintain the company's success: the Blue Bell family. At every critical moment of the company's history the well-being of employees has been factored into the decisions made.

Rather than lay folks off in response to tough times, the directors generated ideas to increase income. At one point they considered producing cheese, a natural adjunct to the butter and ice cream businesses. A cheese plant in Cameron, Texas, had halted production and was ripe for acquisition. The Blue Bell board studied this proposition thoroughly but for reasons unknown eventually decided against it. But they did choose to step up sales by providing surplus butter to Borden's Produce Company of Houston.

Supplemental Sales

Still, the most profitable prospect seemed to be retail sales of ice cream. Blue Bell Creameries established Lotta Cream stores in several locations to sell ice cream by the cone. Lotta Cream #1 appeared inside Mr. Schmid's store in Brenham early in 1935, when Blue Bell sold double-dip ice cream cones for a nickel each. On a typical Saturday in Brenham, customers at Lotta Cream #1 consumed 110 gallons of ice cream.

Pleased with good profits from Lotta Cream #1, Blue Bell quickly established ice cream booths inside businesses in nearby towns. Lotta Cream stores appeared in Elgin, Smithville, Giddings, Taylor, La Grange, Navasota, and Bastrop. Until home refrigerators with freezing compartments became available, ice cream parlors, booths, and soda fountains provided the most convenient way for people to purchase Blue Bell Ice Cream. The advent of double-dip cones sweetened the enterprise of buying and selling ice cream for everyone.

Barnhill's Drugstore in the First National Bank Building in Brenham also sold Blue Bell Ice Cream. Its state-of-the-art soda fountain was installed in 1930. The fountain, with a Vitrolite counter, featured electrical refrigeration and maintained five different temperature settings to keep ice cream, syrups, dairy products, and other ingredients at proper levels of coldness. What must have seemed like mile-high cones and other frozen concoctions no doubt provided Brenhamites a bit of cool, if temporary, respite from the difficulties of the Great Depression.

Modern Equipment

With sales on the upswing, E. F. Kruse recognized the inklings of a turnaround in the economy and prepared for the future. In 1936 he recommended that the creamery purchase its first refrigerated truck to supply the growing market more efficiently. With board approval, he bought a one-and-a-half-ton 1933 Chevrolet truck from Schawe Motor Company. The refrigerated body of the truck came from American Body Works in Dallas. This vehicle held 20 five-gallon cans of ice cream and delivered to Lotta Cream stores, soda fountains, and drugstores within a thirty-five-mile radius of Brenham.

Still thinking ahead, E.F. further demonstrated his positive outlook for the creamery when he acquired a direct expansion freezer from the Southern Dairy Supply Company in 1937. Rather than producing ice cream in twenty-gallon batches, like the company's other freezers, this machine emitted a one-inch stream at the rate of eighty-five gallons per hour. Even E.F. expressed amazement at Blue Bell's first true continuous freezer: "Who will be able to eat all of that ice cream?"

Other purchases indicating a rosy future for Blue Bell Creameries included a larger Vilter ice machine, a new truck for Giddings, and, last but not least, a cash register. The company also began filling pint-size containers in anticipation of the increased consumption of ice cream sure to come with household refrigerators. It's no wonder that the board voted to increase E.F.'s salary twice before the close of the decade. By the end of 1939 he was worth every penny of his $225 monthly salary.

Despite the pinch felt by all during the Great Depression, Blue Bell Creameries managed to emerge from the 1930s in a position to expand its business. Who knew that World War II was on the horizon?

Ice Cream Cone, Ralph Smith Photography

Bullets

Fruit-flavored bullet on a stick, available in cherry, orange, lime, or grape . . .
—From an in-house description of Blue Bell's Bullet

At the beginning of the 1940s, Blue Bell Creameries produced six flavors of ice cream: vanilla, chocolate, strawberry, buttered pecan, banana nut, and tutti-frutti. Vanilla, a perennial favorite, accounted for 45 percent of the ice cream sales. Of course, Blue Bell continued to manufacture butter in both Brenham and Giddings.

As far as frozen snacks were concerned, Blue Bell made its own ice cream sandwiches, but the Popsicles®, Dreamsicles®, and Fudgsicles® it produced were under the auspices of the Joe Lowe Corporation of New York. Joe Lowe provided the Popsicle® Corporation's recipes, ingredients, molds, sticks, and wrappers. Blue Bell handled manufacturing and distribution. In this manner the Popsicle® Corporation's novelties became available in Central Texas.

Dirty White Uniforms

Driver salesmen wore white uniforms in the '40s and '50s. Mrs. Agnes Anderson, widow of Elton B. "Andy" Anderson (employed 1930–1983), recalled how dirty those uniforms became. Blue Bell sold bulk ice cream in five- or ten-gallon metal cans. When the driver salesmen retrieved those containers from their customers, melted ice cream often remained inside. Rainwater also found its way into the cans that store owners placed by the back door for Blue Bell personnel to pick up. When the salesmen threw the "empty" cans into the truck for the journey back to Brenham, they were splashed with the contents. Mrs. Anderson soaked the white uniforms for twelve hours before washing them in hot, soapy water, using a brush and a scrub board. Thankfully, heavy-duty washing machines were in her future.

Kruse Children

Summertime production of ice cream and novelties created the need for part-time employees. In 1941 E.F. hired his thirteen-year-old son, Ed., and his eleven-year-old son, Howard, to work in the plant during their school break. Two of E.F.'s three daughters, Bertha and Mildred, also pitched in at the creamery by working either in production or in the office. Evelyn Ann, the youngest of the five Kruse children, remained at home with her mother, Bertha.

That first summer in the plant left lasting impressions on Ed. and Howard, especially in terms of their firsthand experience of their father's work ethic. E.F. arrived before the other employees and locked the door on his way out at the end of the day. Believing that "idle hands were the devil's workshop," he required the boys to work eight hours a day, six days a week during the summers. As a result, the boys began developing good work habits of their own.

Youthful Contributions

The boys also learned to appreciate the value of one thin dime. E.F. paid them ten cents per hour at the plant, and Ed. and Howard labored hard to earn their eighty cents a day. One of their tasks involved making ice cream sandwiches. Taking a tray of frozen vanilla ice cream from the freezer, the boys divided the block into 64 four-ounce rectangles with a knife, placed each rectangle of ice cream between two chocolate wafers, wrapped the resulting sandwich in paper, and placed it in a box for delivery. Other routine tasks included wrapping pounds of butter or inserting sticks in the frozen novelties.

One of the less pleasant chores was scouring empty ice cream cans. Because these five- and ten-gallon containers returned from retail outlets dirty, crusty, and sour-smelling, they required a thorough cleaning. It was a difficult task, second in popularity only to peeling peaches. Removing the skin from the fruit took little effort, but removing the itchy peach fuzz from one's own skin was an entirely different matter. Fortunately for the boys, Blue Bell made peach ice cream only when the company could procure ripe Texas peaches, which was during a very short period in the summer.

Just Desserts

The $4.80 per week that each of the boys earned had to be carefully distributed. They each paid $2.75 of their weekly income to their mother for groceries and a nickel to Uncle

Creamery-Packed Carton

In the late 1940s consumers could purchase cartons of Blue Bell Ice Cream and store them in the freezer compartments of their new refrigerators.

Hohlt's

Opposite page: A 1944 artistic depiction of Brenham's Main Street focused on Hohlt's department store. Owner H. F. Hohlt was an original founder of the Brenham Creamery Company. He held the title of president of the company from 1919 to 1931. His son Herbert C. Hohlt was president of Blue Bell Creameries from 1931 to 1968.

A Different View

Following page: The entrance to the offices of the Little Creamery in Brenham features Art Deco architecture.

Cash Report Ledger

The records for the Brenham
Creamery Company date back
to the 1920s.

Chest-Style Home Freezer

Opposite page: After many years
of deprivation brought about by
the Great Depression and World
War II, the U.S. economy began to
boom. In the late 1940s consumers
could enjoy eating their Blue Bell
Ice Cream at home in a leisurely
fashion. New appliances with
freezing capabilities made this
luxury possible.

Sam for Social Security taxes. E.F. allowed his sons to keep the remaining $2.00. Ed. likes to say he spent his gains somewhat freely, unlike Howard, who probably placed his net profit in a savings account where it continues to accumulate interest even today.

It wasn't all work and no play, though. Ed. and Howard found plenty of ways to amuse themselves during their days at the plant. Scraping frozen ice off the pipes, the boys managed to have snowball fights—a relief during the hot Central Texas summers before air-conditioning. If E.F. knew about the snow in July, he said nothing. However, the sight of Ed. and his friend Tony Zientek engaged in butter combat resulted in a spanking. Ice from the pipes had no retail value; throwing away butter was playing with profits.

Valuable Lessons

Between spills and chills, Ed. and Howard learned much about making ice cream from their father, an effective teacher. They grew to respect and emulate the Christian principles their father applied to his personal and business life. That E.F. lived the Golden Rule was not lost on his sons, whose list of virtues for their father includes ethical, hardworking, straightforward, fair-minded, practical, self-motivated, trustworthy, innovative, and frugal. The boys learned well the lessons of their mentor, as is evident in the knowledge, values, and practices they've passed on to succeeding generations of Blue Bell employees.

End of Innocence

The summer of 1941, their first at the creamery, remains vivid in the minds of Ed. and Howard Kruse, but December 7, 1941, made an indelible impression on them and everyone else at the company. When the Japanese attacked Pearl Harbor, Blue Bell, like the rest of the country, immediately mobilized for World War II. The 1941 Christmas bonus for company employees included $25 cash and a $25 war bond. The creamery concentrated its efforts on manufacturing butter for the troops. According to Ed. Kruse, "We would literally make railcars and truckloads of butter and ship them off to military installations like Fort Hood in Killeen for the soldiers."

Once again times grew tough, and the creamery found it necessary to borrow money several times during the war. Seldom do the company's board minutes make reference to world events, but World War II was an exception: "A heavy inventory of supplies for manufacture of our products must be carried on account of the present world conditions."

Desperate Measures

With limited amounts of butterfat available for ice cream, Blue Bell focused on manufacturing sherbets. Sherbets contain only 1 to 2 percent milkfat and are lighter and sweeter than ice cream. When sugar rationing became part of the war effort, the creamery switched to alternative sweeteners, such as honey, syrup, and even dark Karo syrup. The resulting concoction, called Frozette, failed to meet the high standards of Blue Bell. On those rare occasions when authentic ice cream did become available, Blue Bell reluctantly required customers to purchase three cans of Frozette to get one container of the real deal. Furthermore, the rationing of tires and gasoline caused delivery problems for the creamery, while a scarcity of equipment for purchase made it difficult to increase butter production for the troops.

As always, Blue Bell soldiered on, doing the best it could under rationing constraints and wage and price controls. When able-bodied employees enlisted or were drafted, the workers left at the company were either under seventeen, over thirty-six, or otherwise deemed unfit for service. Those in the plant during the war labored between fifty and eighty hours per week and earned only $15 to $25. The company's hands were tied, for the U.S. government required that the Salary Stabilization Unit approve all salaries and bonuses. The war effort succeeded, but the economy stagnated.

As the victorious troops returned home in late 1945, business was ready to boom. E.F. and the board of directors pledged to plow any surplus proceeds back into the plant to compensate for the necessary neglect during the war. By the end of 1949, Blue Bell Creameries had built a new office addition to the front of the plant and a two-story stucco warehouse, paved the street leading to the creamery, updated and improved equipment, and added more trucks to its fleet.

Meanwhile, American consumers repaid themselves for sacrifices endured during the war years and began making significant purchases—homes, automobiles, and major appliances. The availability of modern refrigerators with freezing compartments appealed to growing families. Made safer and less expensive because of the coolant Freon, refrigerator-freezers found their way into millions of homes. The demand for Blue Bell Ice Cream increased rapidly as families in Central Texas enjoyed their frozen desserts at home.

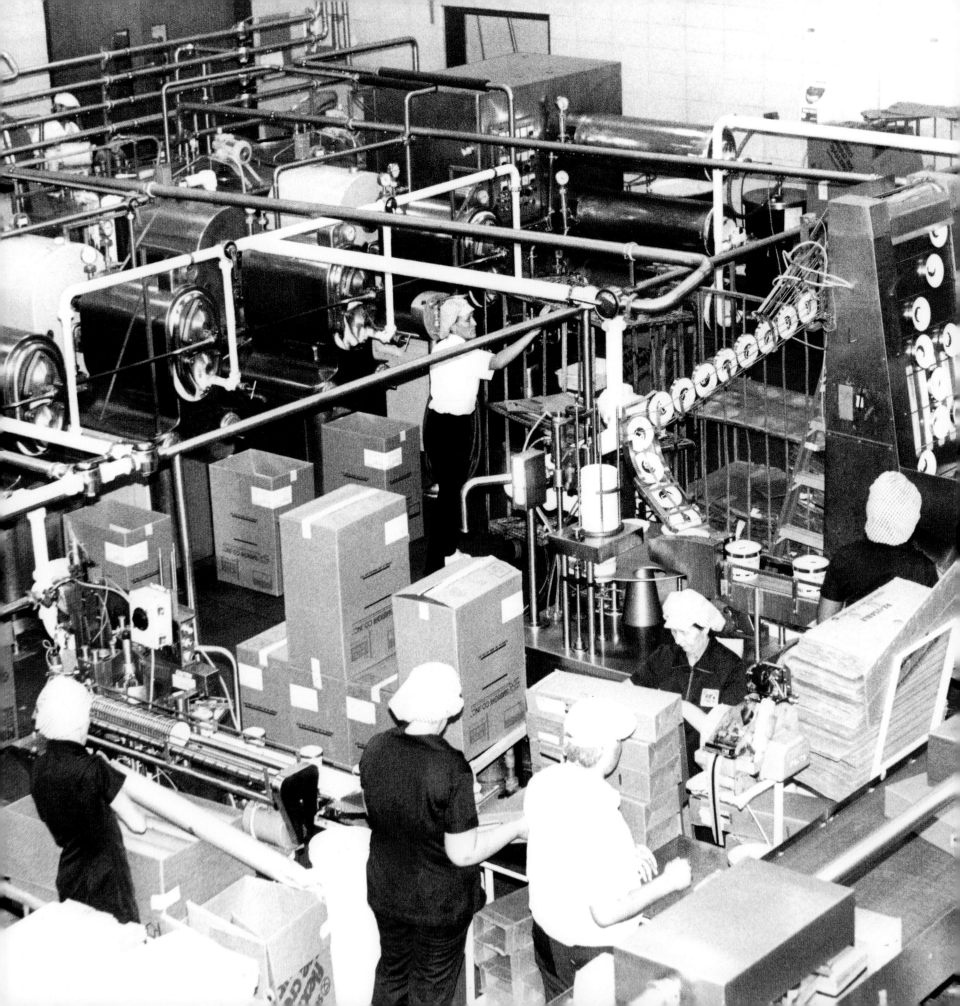

How Do We Make Ice Cream?

Consumers often ask how Blue Bell makes "the best ice cream in the country." According to Howard Kruse, the secret lies in the company's deep commitment to quality and consistency. The actual recipe requires more than three thousand of the most dedicated and knowledgeable employees in the industry. Next come the finest ingredients available, the cleanest and most efficient equipment, and the most time-honored processes. Also needed is the closest monitoring of temperatures. And, of course, the freshest development of new products is a must. Only with these assets is Blue Bell able to live up to its slogan and guarantee that each new spoonful of your favorite flavor of Blue Bell Ice Cream tastes as delicious as the last.

The following two pages illustrate how Blue Bell makes ice cream. Remember that throughout each step in the entire process, Blue Bell personnel are ensuring that the company's highest standards are met.

Opposite page: A bird's-eye view of production and packaging processes in Brenham.

How Ice Cream Is Homemade at Blue Bell

1 **MILK TANKS**
Would you believe it takes two huge, 40,000-gallon tanks just to store our milk? That keeps dairy farmers around Brenham fairly busy, because we need fresh milk nearly every day. We also have two 6,000-gallon tanks for storing fresh cream. These ingredients flow to a mixing room, where we begin the blending and cooking of Blue Bell Ice Cream.

2 **MIXING ROOM**
Ever wonder why our ice cream is so rich? Because pure cane sugar, corn syrup, milk, and cream are the main ingredients. We blend them in 2,000-gallon tanks, and this basic mix is used for most of our ice creams. The different flavorings will be added later.

3 **PASTEURIZER**
Did you know the milk you drink has been heated to kill the germs in it? The process is called pasteurization, and we do the same thing to our ice cream. Our basic mix flows into heating tubes, where we heat it to 180° Fahrenheit for 26 seconds. The heat kills any harmful germs that might be present, and then the mix is ready for the next step.

4 **HOMOGENIZER**
Curious about what makes Blue Bell Ice Cream so smooth? Homogenization has a lot to do with it. The mix flows into our homogenizer, where more than 2,000 pounds of pressure are put on it. This weight crushes the tiny drops of milkfat in the mix, making them even smaller. And that makes our ice cream smoother than ever.

5 **PLATE COOLER**
Now we're ready to begin cooling the hot mix. It flows into our plate cooler, where the mix temperature is lowered to about 35° Fahrenheit. That's just a few degrees above freezing, so the mix still flows easily. It's stored at this temperature before going on to be flavored.

6 **FLAVORING TANKS**
Dark chocolate from Holland, pure peppermint oil costing more than $200 a gallon, and other delicious flavorings make this the tastiest part of our whole operation. Suppose we want to make strawberry ice cream. Strawberry flavoring is added to the mix, along with fresh strawberry juice. The actual strawberries will be added in the next step.

7 **FREEZER BARRELS**
Now the mix is whipped and frozen in special cooling barrels. As it leaves the barrels, our people add fruits and nuts to flavors that require them. Top-grade spring strawberries, Elberta and Rio Oso peaches, and native Texas pecans are typical of Blue Bell's farm-fresh ingredients.

8 **FILLING OPERATIONS**
We fill all kinds of containers with Blue Bell products. Half-gallon- and pint-sized cartons are filled with ice cream, and some of our frozen snacks are also wrapped here. Next, they all ride a conveyor belt into our hardening room.

9 **HARDENING ROOM**
It's so cold in here, employees dress like Eskimos. Would you believe it's -20° Fahrenheit? The low temperature helps us to freeze the ice cream quickly, while it's still smooth and creamy. Then it's ready for delivery to your neighborhood store.

10 **ICE CREAM TRUCKS**
When you're getting out of bed in the morning, we're already on the road with fresh ice cream for your store. After arriving, our driver packs the freezer himself to make sure it's neat, well stocked, and filled with all of your favorite flavors of Blue Bell Ice Cream.

Opposite page: Blue Bell had this poster commissioned in 1985 to describe the process for making its ice cream.

HOW ICE CREAM IS HOMEMADE AT BLUE BELL®

In the early days, making ice cream was pretty easy at Blue Bell. Our biggest piece of equipment was an old tub filled with crushed ice. This was back in 1911, when making two gallons of ice cream was a busy day for us.

Now we're making millions of gallons a year, and our equipment has become more complicated. But you know something? Our ice cream still has old-timey flavor.

So let's get cooking, and see how the Blue Bell folks turn cow's milk into delicious, homemade-tasting ice cream.

1 MILK TANKS

Would you believe it takes two huge, 40,000-gallon tanks just to store our milk? That keeps dairy farmers around Brenham fairly busy, because we need fresh milk nearly every day. We also have two 6,000-gallon tanks for storing fresh cream. These ingredients flow to a mixing room, where we begin the blending and cooking of Blue Bell Ice Cream.

2 MIXING ROOM

Ever wonder why our ice cream is so rich? Because pure cane sugar, corn syrup, milk and cream are the main ingredients. We blend them in 2,000-gallon tanks, and this basic mix is used for most of our ice creams. The different flavorings will be added later.

3 PASTEURIZER

Did you know the milk you drink has been heated to kill the germs in it? We do the same thing to our ice cream, and the process is called pasteurization. Our basic mix flows into heating tubes, where we heat it to 180° Farenheit for 26 seconds. The heat kills any harmful germs if they are present, and then the mix is ready for the next step.

4 HOMOGENIZER

Curious about what makes Blue Bell Ice Cream so smooth? Homogenization has a lot to do with it. The mix flows into our homogenizer, where over 2,000 pounds of pressure is put on it. This weight crushes tiny drops of milkfat in the mix, making them even smaller. And that makes our ice cream smoother than ever.

5 PLATE COOLER

Now we're ready to begin cooling the hot mix. It flows into our plate cooler, where the mix temperature is lowered to about 35° Farenheit. That's just a few degrees above freezing, so the mix still flows easily. It's stored at this temperature before going on to be flavored.

6 FLAVORING TANKS

Dark chocolate from Holland, pure peppermint oil costing over $200 a gallon, and other delicious flavorings make this the tastiest part of our whole operation. Suppose we want to make strawberry ice cream? Strawberry flavoring is now added to the mix, along with fresh strawberry juice. The actual strawberries will be added in the next step.

7 FREEZER BARRELS

Now the mix is whipped and frozen in special cooling barrels. And as it leaves the barrels, our people add fruits and nuts to flavors that require them. Top-grade spring strawberries, Elberta and Rio Oso peaches, and native Texas pecans are typical of Blue Bell's farm-fresh ingredients.

8 FILLING OPERATIONS

We fill all kinds of containers with Blue Bell products. Half-gallon, quart and pint-sized cartons are filled with ice cream, and some of our frozen snacks are also wrapped here. Next, they all ride a conveyor belt into our hardening room.

9 HARDENING ROOM

It's so cold in here, men dress like Eskimos. Would you believe it's 20° Farenheit below zero? The low temperature helps us to freeze the ice cream quickly, while it's still smooth and creamy. Then it's ready for delivery to your neighborhood store.

10 ICE CREAM TRUCKS

When you're getting out of bed in the morning, we're already on the road with fresh ice cream for your store. After arriving, our driver packs the freezer himself to make sure it's neat, well stocked, and filled with all of your favorite flavors of Blue Bell Ice Cream.

Dos
Amigos

*The unique flavoring of Mexican vanilla swirled with a Mexican chocolate
ice cream that has a hint of cinnamon . . .*
—From an in-house description of Blue Bell's Dos Amigos flavor

As the new decade began, E. F. Kruse responded to changing trends by experimenting further with small containers, not only pints but quarts and half gallons, which would fit easily into the modern refrigerators. In another stroke of brilliance, he developed a program to provide freezer cabinets to grocers, so consumers could buy their ice cream and frozen snacks when and where they bought their groceries.

With the growth Blue Bell was experiencing and the booming numbers of retail outlets for the creamery's products, E.F. might have needed assistance from his sons, but he wasn't ready to ask for it. Despite the fact that Ed. had graduated from Texas A&M with a bachelor's degree in dairy manufacturing in 1949, E.F. had not planned for him to join the company after graduation. Since Ed. had been a member of the Aggie Corps of Cadets, E.F. expected him to accept a two-year commission in the U.S. Army, but as it happened, in 1949 the army did not need college graduates with officer training. Because E.F. did not have a position for him, Ed. went to work with Swift and Company as an outside salesman in the company's Fort Worth ice cream division.

Ed. gained valuable experience in selling and distributing ice cream products during his time with Swift, the fourth-largest ice cream manufacturer in the United States. He progressed rapidly through the ranks to become the branch manager at Swift's Corsicana distribution center, then returned to Fort Worth as the sales representative for the western half of the city. However, a disturbing lack of teamwork among the Swift employees, their seeming disinterest in each other's welfare, and their sense of disconnection from the company's success made a deeply negative impression on Ed.

A Lesson in Ethics

Ed. F. Kruse was only twenty-three years old when his father died and he assumed management of Blue Bell Creameries. Ed. deemed purchasing to be his weak suit, but he caught on fairly quickly. E. F. Kruse had worked out deals with three companies with which Blue Bell did business. Blue Bell received a discount of 2 percent on purchases and had thirty days to pay its bills. Shortly after Ed. took charge, one of the vendors rescinded the 2 percent discount. Soon the second supplier did the same thing. When the third began discussing reducing the discount, Ed. looked at him defiantly, and the vendor changed his mind. At that point Ed. quit doing business with the other two companies. When their representatives offered to reinstate the discounts, Ed. did not relent. He refused to do business with people who took advantage of his youth and inexperience. Integrity is a valuable commodity in the world of business.

Father and Son Together

When Ed. visited his parents in Brenham in early 1951, his mother told him that E.F. needed help at the creamery. Ed. expressed willingness to join Blue Bell if E.F. would simply ask him, but Bertha explained that his father had too much pride to do that. Bertha finally broke the impasse by bringing the two men together, ostensibly to discuss staffing issues at the creamery. As a result, Ed. began working as a Blue Bell route supervisor in February 1951.

Ed.'s duties at Blue Bell were similar to those he had had at Swift. He drove a white panel truck to make sales calls and set up advertising displays in stores. Little did he realize that his duties would expand exponentially before the end of the year.

E.F.'s Unexpected Death

As Ed. explains, "In the fall of 1951, my father began to have some pains in his side and became ill. The doctors diagnosed him with cancer and chose to operate. They found cancer of the stomach that had spread to his duodenum and appendix. Two weeks after the operation, an infection set in, and he passed away on October 21."

In shock and dismay, the Kruse family, Blue Bell Creameries, and the entire community of Brenham endeavored to cope

Blue Bell Logo

During most of the fifties, sixties, and seventies, this bell image represented Blue Bell Creameries.

Ed. F. Kruse at 21

Opposite page: Ed. Kruse, a member of the Corps of Cadets, graduated from Texas A&M in 1949.

Blue Bell Sales Department

Following page: In 1958 the Blue Bell sales force posed in front of their fleet. From left to right are territory managers Vastine Pietsch, Marvin Giese, and Elton "Andy" Anderson. Next to them are driver salesmen Alvin Hueske, Erich Jaster, Raymond Warmke, Roland Harbers, Carl Meier, Wilfred Meier, Clarence Jaster, Collin Pietsch, Floyd Stegent, and Wilbert "Buddy" Meier.

Brenham, Texas, Oct 31, 1955

Mr Buddy Meier

IN ACCOUNT WITH

BLUE BELL CREAMERIES
B. B. ICE CREAM
AND BLUE BELL BUTTER

TERMS: PHONES   BRENHAM 2777 GIDDINGS 6

Oct 1 | To Balance | 114 00
By cash | 13 00
| 101 00

Salary Receipt

Wilbert "Buddy" Meier began working as a driver salesman in 1955. He earned $114 in October of that year.

Early Mellorine Carton

At right: Blue Bell began producing mellorine in 1952.

Howard at Work

Opposite page: When Howard Kruse joined Blue Bell Creameries on a full-time basis in 1954, he set his sights on production.

Bluebells

Following page: The purplish wildflowers flourish in the heat of the summer in Central Texas—about the same time ice cream is most appreciated.

with the loss of their much loved and esteemed husband, father, leader, mayor pro tem, and fellow citizen. Carrying on as duty required, all those touched by E. F. Kruse's life slowly came to grips with the implications of his untimely death.

Stepping Up to the Plate

For several weeks, Blue Bell's president, Herbert Hohlt, and the other members of the board of directors made no effort to find a manager to replace E.F. It wasn't until mid-November that Ed. Kruse asked Hohlt if the company would consider him for the position. Hohlt explained to Ed. that the board had been giving him time to grieve for his father but had hoped he would want the job. On November 16, 1951, at age twenty-three (the same age as E.F. was when he accepted the managerial position at the Brenham Creamery Company), Ed. Kruse took charge as manager, secretary, and treasurer of Blue Bell Creameries.

Despite his youth, Ed. had the perfect educational background for his new position, he brought knowledge from his job at Swift, and he knew well the procedures and personnel at Blue Bell from his work in the plant during summers, holidays, and weekends. What he didn't know, he would learn—even if it meant he had to work twenty-four hours a day to do it. Especially on the inevitable bad days when he faced total exhaustion, Ed. remained motivated to prove to his father that he would not fail the creamery. E.F. had often warned his sons about second generations who had bankrupted the solid companies their fathers had established. Ed. Kruse was determined to succeed.

Taking Charge

Ed. hit the ground running. One of his first decisions was to manufacture mellorine, a frozen dessert made very inexpensively from vegetable oil. Not only had E.F. refused to make this non-dairy product, but he competed with ice cream makers who did by reducing the price of his ice cream. Ed. quickly deduced that his father's approach lost the company money. Under his direction Blue Bell began manufacturing a tasty mellorine that measured up not only to the flavors but also to the costs and prices of the competitors' mellorine products.

Ed. also courted success at the other end of the spectrum, with the richest ice cream the company had yet produced: Blue Bell Supreme. Ed. insisted that this premium brand be made with only the best sweet cream and milk products available. In an effort to further distinguish the line, Ed. priced it higher than the competition's products and packaged it in distinctive pints and half gallons designed for home use.

Ed. applied himself equally inventively to other aspects of the business. He added a new hardening room and bar tank to the plant and purchased an ice cream freezer and a refrigerated truck. His efforts were rewarded; at the end of his first full year as manager, Blue Bell's bottom line lay decidedly in the black. His strategy of increasing sales to compensate for some of his possible shortcomings as a manager had worked. Realizing that he had met all of his responsibilities to the company and its thirty-five employees and their families, the young Ed. Kruse shed tears of relief and gratitude.

Hiring Howard

In 1953 Blue Bell embarked upon a major plant expansion designed to manufacture its fifty products more efficiently. Ed.'s confidence as a manager (not to mention his push for success) received a tremendous boost when his brother, Howard, joined Blue Bell in 1954. In 1952 Howard had earned his own bachelor's degree in dairy manufacturing from Texas A&M. Which isn't to say that Ed. and Howard claim to have had the same college experience. Ed. likes to point out that while he knew every person on the Texas A&M campus by name, Howard achieved the highest grade point average ever in the school's dairy science major—2.93 on a 3.0 scale.

When he graduated, Howard was drafted, as were all military school graduates at the time. Although he arrived in Korea

Following page photo: Bluebells. Fayette County. Richard Reynolds

only five days before the war ended, Howard remained there for a year as an advisory officer to the Republic of Korea. Upon leaving the army in 1954, he immediately began what turned out to be a fifty-plus-year career at Blue Bell.

Dual Purposes

The brothers' complementary strengths have served the company well. While Ed. focused on sales, personnel, and administrative issues, Howard set his sights on fine-tuning the operations of the plant. He expanded upon his education and experience at the creamery with a practical, hands-on approach to learning everything about making ice cream. Three areas drew his close attention. As he had always found milk to be the world's perfect food, he especially enjoyed experimenting with it in the lab and developing a variety of delicious ice cream blends. Moving from art into science, he relished refining plant processes and procedures and then

Miss Annie

Annie Spinn Neumann enlivened Brenham as one of the community's eccentrics. For more than fifty years, she drove the four miles into town from her small farm to sell excess cream to Blue Bell Creameries. Her mode of transportation, even in the late 1950s, was a horse and buggy. Miss Annie also sold butter and eggs to various customers in Brenham. Oddly, Miss Annie never stepped out of her carriage. She yelled to her customers to come get their products from her cart. If she needed items herself, she stopped in front of a store and beckoned a clerk to come outside to serve her. Miss Annie insisted on top service and the highest quality in all her purchases.

For some reason, every citizen in town respected Miss Annie's demands—including the automobile drivers who collectively sighed through the traffic jams she caused with her horse and buggy.

buying or adapting machinery to better manufacture ice cream and frozen snacks to Blue Bell's strict specifications. Finally, he drew a bead on quality control. Soon he became known as "the demandingest man in Washington County," for he accepted nothing less than the best when it came to making Blue Bell's ice cream: the freshest and finest ingredients, knowledgeable employees, effective methods of preventing heat shock (partial thawing and refreezing, which detrimentally affects texture) to the products, and the cleanest, most efficient, and most innovative plant possible.

The decade that suddenly introduced the second generation of Kruse management and Blue Bell Supreme Ice Cream also brought women working in plant production for the first time (1951), the closing of the Giddings branch of Blue Bell Creameries to consolidate operations (1956), the establishment of pension and hospitalization plans for employees (1957 and 1959, respectively), and the decision to stop making butter (1958) in order to utilize all the available sweet cream for the manufacture of ice cream. In 1957 Blue Bell Creameries celebrated its fiftieth anniversary and resolutely extended its charter with the State of Texas for another fifty years. The future looked bright.

Point-of-Purchase Signs

These banners appeared in stores where Blue Bell Ice Cream was sold in the 1950s.

50th Anniversary Photograph

Opposite page: Kervin Finke, retired snack plant manager, began working at Blue Bell in 1956. He remembers the summer day in 1957 when Blue Bell invited visitors to tour the plant as part of its fiftieth anniversary celebration. Production went on as usual all day, but at 5:00 p.m. people began coming in to watch the manufacturing process. They seemed very interested in the methods employed and asked many questions. In addition to the tour, Blue Bell celebrated by raffling off a chest-style freezer. The visitors also received free "nickel" cups of ice cream at the end of the tour. Kervin doesn't remember how many people viewed the plant that evening, but he does recall that the used nickel cups filled five or six drums. The entire workforce also posed for a photograph that day.

Ed. F. Kruse

Edward Fred "Ed." Kruse was born on March 15, 1928, in Brenham, Texas, the third child of E. F. and Bertha (Quebe) Kruse. Reared in Brenham, he attended Brenham High School and served as co-captain of the football and basketball teams.

He was senior class president in 1945 and went on to complete his formal education at Texas A&M University in College Station, where he was recognized as a distinguished military student in the Corps of Cadets. He also lettered on the varsity swim team in 1948–1949. He earned a B.S. degree in dairy manufacturing upon graduating in 1949.

Although associated with Blue Bell Creameries since the age of thirteen, Ed. joined the company on a full-time basis in 1951 as a sales supervisor. That same year, his father, E.F., died, and Ed. assumed his father's position as manager and secretary/treasurer. In 1968 he was named chairman, president, and general manager of Blue Bell Creameries, and in 1986 chief executive officer. In 1993 Ed. moved into a part-time role with the company, but he remains chairman of the board.

Ed. F. Kruse has served on the Texas Lutheran College Board of Regents, and he received an honorary doctorate there in 2001. He has also served as chairman of the Lutheran Foundation of the Southwest. He is a past president of the Brenham Industrial Foundation, the Brenham Rotary Club, the Dairy Products Institute of Texas, the Dixie Dairy Products Association, and St. Paul's Evangelical Lutheran Church in Brenham. He is past chairman of the board of MBank in Brenham and of the International Association of Ice Cream Manufacturers.

In 1987 Ed. was named Washington County Man of the Year, and he was inducted into the Texas Business Hall of Fame in 1993. In 1995 he was named Lutheran of the Year by the Lutheran Social Services of the South and was inducted into the Dairy Products Institute of Texas Hall of Fame. In 1998 he received the Soaring Eagle Award from the International Ice Cream Association for service above and beyond the call of duty. In 2002 he received the Outstanding Philanthropist Award from the National Agricultural Alumni and Development Association and the 2002 Texas A&M College of Agriculture and Life Sciences Outstanding Alumni Award. In October 2003 Ed. was inducted into the Texas A&M Corps of Cadets Hall of Honor. The following year, he became a Distinguished Alumnus of Brenham High School. In 2005 Texas A&M University selected him as a Distinguished Alumnus, and that same year, he and his brother, Howard W. Kruse, received the Ernst and Young Entrepreneur of the Year Award.

Ed. Kruse is married to the former Evelyn Tiaden. They had four children, Karen, Ken (deceased), Paul, and Neil (deceased). Ed. and Evelyn are also the proud grandparents of twenty-one grandchildren. Ed. is an avid golfer and saltwater fisherman.

Homemade Vanilla

Rich, homemade-tasting vanilla ice cream with a special hand-cranked flavor that's the best in the country . . .
—From an in-house description of Blue Bell's Homemade Vanilla flavor

During its first fifty years of producing ice cream, Blue Bell Creameries had steadily grown to encompass all of Brenham and the surrounding Central Texas communities in its sales territory. Now the company serviced accounts on the outskirts of Houston.

In 1960 Houston ranked as the seventh-largest city in the United States, with a population of just under one million people and with more newcomers arriving every day. Ed. Kruse realized that his consumer base in Central Texas would drop with the population shift from smaller towns to larger cities. If he wanted to continue to grow Blue Bell, his company would have to sell ice cream where the people were moving.

Considering Houston

How could a small-town concern compete in the big city? Houstonians certainly suffered no shortage of ice cream. Companies such as Carnation, Borden, Lilly, Swift, and Foremost Dairies furnished ample supplies. Having worked for Swift and having studied the Houston market specifically, Ed. knew exactly how Blue Bell surpassed these well-known manufacturers. First, Blue Bell produced an ice cream of consistently superior taste and quality compared to that available from the larger companies. Next, Blue Bell route salesmen provided praiseworthy service to their accounts and delivered their products in prime condition. Finally, small-town values permeated the company— the workers were friendly, honest, and above all, enthusiastic. With those qualities and teamwork, Blue Bell could be successful in the highly competitive Houston market.

Hiring John Barnhill

The key to the operation's success would rest with the person representing the company in the Houston territory. Ed. wanted John W. Barnhill, Jr., for the job. The fact that John held a journalism position at the *Houston Press* did not deter Ed. from pursuing him. He wooed John with countless cajoling letters until John agreed to join the team.

No small part of Barnhill's appeal was that he was a hometown boy. He had grown up in Brenham. His father, a pharmacist, sold Blue Bell products in his Barnhill's Drugstores and currently sat on the company's board of directors. John Jr., like so many other Brenham teens, had received his "baptism by fire" in the working world during summer employment at Blue Bell. Remembering how the teenaged John broke a toe one summer by dropping a ten-gallon ice cream can on his foot, Ed. Kruse would forever after deem John unfit for a manufacturing position. The mishap did not otherwise hamper John's career, however. He had graduated with a journalism degree from The University of Texas, served in the armed forces, and worked as an assistant to George Christian, who later became President Lyndon B. Johnson's press secretary. Ed. knew that John W. Barnhill, Jr., exhibited the intelligence, people skills, and work ethic that could break open the Houston market.

John's Persistence

When John began making his sales calls in Houston in 1960, Blue Bell had thirteen accounts on the outskirts of the city. John's job consisted of servicing those accounts—two of the early customers were tiny stores named Joe's and Tony's— and developing new ones. Every day John carried ice cream samples to convenience stores and mom-and-pop grocery stores in an effort to persuade the owners to make room for Blue Bell in their freezer cases. Consumers who tried Blue Bell products liked them and began to spread the word. After work, John assumed the role of ice cream vendor: He drove a three-wheeled Cushman motor scooter through neighborhoods and sold frozen snacks out of a refrigerated box on the back of it. John literally won Blue Bell devotees one person at a time.

A big break occurred when John scored an appointment to see Sam Sacco, owner of the largest independent grocery

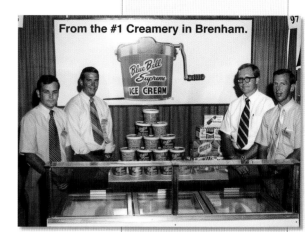

From the #1 Creamery in Brenham.

Future Leaders of Blue Bell

Larry Ainsworth, Melvin Ziegenbein, John Barnhill, and Ray Schomburg promote sales of Blue Bell Ice Cream at a new account in Houston in the 1960s. All four young men would rise to positions of leadership in the company.

Mellorine in the '60s

At left: Mellorine remained a big seller for Blue Bell in the 1960s. Grocery stores sold the vegetable oil–based frozen dessert, charging $1 for three or four half gallons.

Blue Bell Arrives in Houston

Opposite page: Although this photo was taken in the 1980s, it symbolizes Blue Bell's expansion into the Houston area in the early 1960s.

store in Texas. Sacco enjoyed the samples John brought him and ordered enough half gallons to fill a small four-foot freezer case at the rear of his store. Thrilled, John contacted all the Houston relatives of Brenham friends and urged them to shop at Sacco's on Bissonnet. E.F.'s old selling point still held up—they could pick up Blue Bell Ice Cream while they bought other grocery items.

Brisk sales soon prompted Sacco to move the freezer to a more prominent location near the front of his establishment. Dissatisfied that Blue Bell was not in the "official" freezer section with the large Houston ice cream players like Borden and Carnation, John visited Sacco's store every morning to ensure that the Blue Bell freezer was always well stocked. John's service and attention eventually resulted in Blue Bell's presence in the major freezer-aisle cabinet. In the meantime, chains like Weingarten's and Lewis and Coker began to take notice. So did everyone else. Maybe it was because John mentioned Sam Sacco's highly respected name on every sales call he made in Houston.

Vending Machines

Another boon to Houston sales involved Blue Bell's purchase of ninety-one vending machines from the Sun-Up Ice Cream Company, as well as others from South Texas Vendors. These purchases included rights to the existing routes of the companies that were selling the machines. Blue Bell products began to appear in machines all over Houston, especially in the big office buildings downtown. Marvin Giese, who had begun working at Blue Bell in 1934, serviced the vending accounts. The opportunity for consumers to try the company's products expanded, and people began to ask for Blue Bell Ice Cream by name at their grocery stores.

Not surprisingly, the industrious and loyal John Barnhill became the first branch manager in Houston, in 1961. Actually "branch" is a misnomer, since for a time he and Marvin Giese shared space in a tiny metal building that was their office. It sat next to a trailer that served as cold storage for the ice cream. When all the ice cream in the trailer had been dispersed, Marvin would hook up a tractor to it, drive it to Brenham, fill it up, and return with a fresh

load of ice cream to service the growing accounts. Blue Bell began construction of a bona fide branch office building on Karbach Street in 1962.

Ed. Kruse often proclaims: "It's a cinch by the inch but hard by the yard." He explains the adage this way: "If we handle our business well day by day, the future will take care of itself." This slogan applied perfectly to the "invasion" of Houston by Blue Bell Creameries.

Employee Stockholding

Meanwhile, back in Brenham, Ed. recommended to the board of directors that Blue Bell sell stock in the company to employees. Board members agreed that employee ownership in the company would make for more dedicated and committed personnel. The board worked with Sam D. W. Low, a Houston attorney who would soon become a director himself, to take the necessary steps. When the stockholders approved the actions in early 1962, fifteen employees purchased stock through special loans arranged by Ed. Kruse at the First National Bank of Brenham. The interest rate for the notes was 4.8 percent—0.2 percent below the bank's lowest lending rate at the time. Blue Bell's dividends paid 5 percent. The employees would realize a slight profit each year as they paid off their loans and significantly more as they held on to the stock. Throughout the years, Blue Bell continued to encourage employees to invest in the company.

Bare Necessities

When Ed. Kruse sent John Barnhill to the first Houston "branch" in 1960, he simply instructed him to "get all the new business you can." Ed. also provided John with a set of Ed.'s own business cards, which John had to manually correct—with his own name, title, address, and phone number—before handing them to potential customers.

John Barnhill and Marvin Giese, the vending manager, not only officed in the same eight-by-twelve-foot metal building, but they also shared a sturdy secondhand metal desk. John used the drawers on one side, and Marvin, those on the other. The phone sitting in the middle of the desk rang constantly.

The only luxury of that first branch office was the effective window air conditioner—a blessing in Houston's hot, sticky climate.

TONY'S
GROCERY MARKET
B-B ICE CREAM
10 2
Dr Pepper
4
Mary HeLen's
BEAUTY SHOP
HO2-1578
BEER

Capital Decision

As John Barnhill knocked on doors in Houston, opportunity knocked on Ed. Kruse's door. In 1965 Chester Brooks in Austin offered to sell his Lily Fresh company to Blue Bell. Ed. jumped at the chance. Located ninety miles west of Brenham, Austin provided a natural expansion to the company's sales territory. The only person Ed. thought was qualified to head the creamery's second branch was Clarence Jaster, who had been with the company in sales since 1948. Ed. used charm and promises to persuade the reluctant Jaster to accept the position. It was an inspired choice on Ed.'s part: Jaster remained in charge of the successful Austin branch until his retirement in 1994.

Capital Improvements

With the expansion of territory, Howard Kruse labored to keep pace in the plant. During the 1960s he added cold storage, increased manufacturing space, and replaced the concrete floors in the production areas with tile. The creamery now spread over every inch of property available at the Creamery Street location, and the company began looking for land to build a new plant.

Memorable Frozen Snacks

Blue Bell has produced hundreds of different frozen snacks during its century in business. Many of today's products resemble the older ones but have different names or ingredients, because of franchising, jobbing, or trademark issues. Old-timers might enjoy recalling Cho-Chos®, Refreshos®, Baby Ruth Bars®, Drumsticks®, Heath Bars®, Nutty Buddys®, Eskimo Pies®, Big Brown Clowns®, Bomb Pops®, Cherry Merry-Go-Rounds®, and Mouseketeer Bars®.

In the meantime, Howard delighted in acquiring the new equipment that was becoming available in the ice cream industry. In 1965 he installed Blue Bell's first Vitaline. This innovative machine automated the process of manufacturing frozen snacks. It poured mix into molds, sent the molds through brine water to harden the product, and then slightly defrosted the molds with warm water to release the product for bagging. The Vitaline reduced the intensive labor involved in producing frozen snacks and increased the number of items that could be manufactured in a day. Howard added a second Vitaline before the end of the decade, although he literally had to break through existing walls to make space for it.

With the aid of the Vitalines, Blue Bell entered the jobbing business in 1967. This meant that the company sold frozen novelties to other ice cream companies, which in turn sold them to the public. This new direction in creamery sales began with the marketing of the popular frozen Baby Ruth Bar®. Since Blue Bell was the only company in Texas that made the treat, it was available solely in the creamery's sales territory. Ice cream companies in other parts of the state that wanted to offer Baby Ruth Bars® to their customers had to buy the snacks from Blue Bell. The company also jobbed out sales of Popsicles® and Fudgsicles®—especially during the heat of the summer when production at other companies fell short of demand.

Homemade Vanilla Ice Cream

Plant expansion, innovation, and production kept Howard Kruse happy and extremely busy, but he still found time for the most delightful part of his job—developing new ice cream flavors. In 1967 he wondered if he could replicate the flavor of hand-cranked homemade vanilla ice cream. He reveled in this project for almost a year as he experimented with various formulas.

Late in 1968 he felt he had at last hit upon the right combination of texture and flavor, and he tentatively allowed Ed. to test a sample. Ed. agreed that the product tasted as delicious as the old-fashioned hand-cranked ice cream he'd loved as a boy. Howard, still unsure he had hit a home run, ordered only the minimum five thousand cartons for the initial production of Blue Bell's Homemade Vanilla Ice Cream. When this new flavor appeared in the grocery stores in early 1969, cartons flew out of the grocers' freezers. Consumers loved

Slenderette Ice Milk

Blue Bell responded to consumers' requests for a lower-calorie dessert when it produced Slenderette in the 1960s.

They Loved Blue Bell, Yeah, Yeah, Yeah

Opposite page: On August 19, 1965, the Beatles performed to a screaming, ecstatic, sold-out crowd at the Sam Houston Coliseum in Houston. In the audience were 100 fortunate Blue Bell customers who had entered and won a contest for free tickets. Blue Bell may have been a little creamery in the country, but even during the supercharged sixties it kept up with the beat of the times.

it. Since then, Homemade Vanilla Ice Cream has been Blue Bell's best-selling flavor, and its formula is the company's most closely guarded secret.

Advertising to Houstonians

The introduction of Homemade Vanilla Ice Cream alone made 1969 a banner year for the company. However, that year also began the association of Blue Bell Creameries with a small Houston advertising agency owned by Lyle Metzdorf and Clyde Burleson. Blue Bell had never had an advertising budget before moving into Houston. News about the product had spread by word of mouth, through grocery store ads in newspapers, via taste tests in stores, and by hand-painted signs on grocers' plate-glass windows.

As John Barnhill contacted grocers for possible accounts in Houston, he listened to various comments concerning the folly and audacity of a little rural creamery that expected to compete with the big-city ice cream manufacturers. On the other hand, there was the grocer who remarked as he ordered Blue Bell Ice Cream for his store, "If it's being made by those Germans up in Brenham, it must be good."

In a landmark decision, John determined that the company's answer to concerns about the rural creamery should be that Blue Bell produced better ice cream *because* it was made in the country. So he created a radio commercial in which an old-timer reminisced about the good ol' days and the "Little Creamery in Brenham." The approach worked like a charm. Upon hearing the commercial, various ad agencies in the Houston area began vying for the Blue Bell account.

Metzdorf's Contributions

John chose Metzdorf Advertising to handle Blue Bell's ad campaigns because Lyle Metzdorf and Clyde Burleson understood exactly the country image John had in mind. In addition, the two ad men appreciated the fact that Blue Bell Ice Cream really did taste better than the other brands. They felt if they could generate interest enough to get a consumer to try the product once, the ice cream would sell itself from that point on.

So Lyle and Clyde emphasized the gently rolling hills, lush green grass, tranquil Jersey cows, pure babbling brooks, vivid wildflowers, slower-paced rhythms, and friendly, down-to-earth folks in the community of Brenham, where Blue Bell

Ice Cream was made. They also portrayed management as determined to create the best products available.

Metzdorf's first television ad for Blue Bell depicted a family eating Blue Bell Ice Cream on a picnic in the country. When the management of Weingarten's, the largest grocery store chain in Houston, saw the ad, they realized Blue Bell's determination to grow the Houston market. Finally they listened to Blue Bell's sales pitch, sampled the ice cream, and placed the company's products in their stores. After excellent sales at Weingarten's, the other chain stores came on board. John Barnhill, along with new sales representatives Larry Ainsworth

Big Brown Clown

A fun Blue Bell frozen snack, Big Brown Clown was named by the young son of John Barnhill.

Blue Bell Ice Cream on Sale!

Opposite page: Ray Schomburg prepares for a special sale of Blue Bell Ice Cream in the 1960s.

Black Sweet Cherry Ice Cream

Following page: Blue Bell announces a new flavor in the 1960s with a colorful point-of-purchase piece.

Our Favorite Slogans

Lyle Metzdorf enhanced the Little Creamery's image of pastoral bliss with folksy slogans that the public came to love almost as much as they loved Blue Bell Ice Cream itself. Not all of these were keepers, but most are memorable.

"Blue Bell's the best ice cream in the country."

....

"We eat all we can and sell the rest."

....

"Blue Bell's better by a country smile."

....

"We're cranky about flavor."

....

"Cows think Brenham's Heaven."

....

"We took the yuk out of yogurt."

....

"Have yourself a Blue Bell country day."

....

"Blue Bell tastes just like the good old days."

....

"It's a fun thing to eat."

....

"Blue Bell is the state ice cream of Texas."

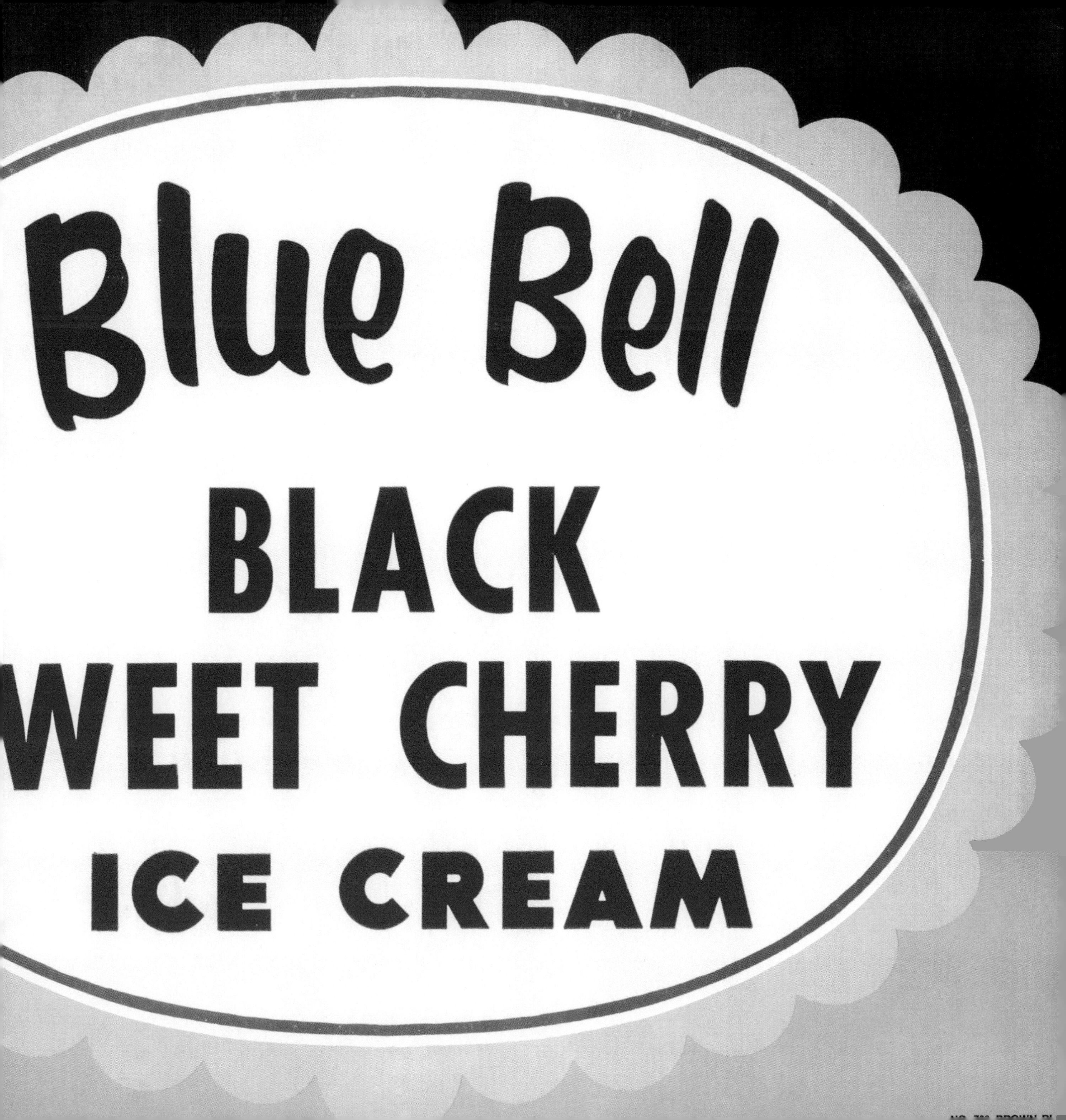
Blue Bell
BLACK
WEET CHERRY
ICE CREAM

and Ray Schomburg, soon sold Blue Bell into virtually the entire Houston market. Customer by customer, store by store, Blue Bell became the number-one-selling ice cream in Houston. A similar scenario unfolded in Austin, where Melvin Ziegenbein joined Clarence Jaster to promote Blue Bell sales in the capital city.

Ed.'s Management Style

Ed. Kruse's ability to find the right person for the right job is legendary at Blue Bell. By merely visiting with a candidate, Ed. reportedly could learn more about that person than the individual knew about himself. Ed. instinctively and confidently hired people who might not yet have the skills the company needed but who demonstrated excellent character,

Drumsticks in the Early Days

"The cones came already formed. We placed thirty-six cones in a basket which held them with pins. The basket had six rows of six cones each. The basket went under a six-row filler, and we flowed vanilla ice cream into each row by using a lever. Then we hand-carried the basket to cold storage. The next day, after the ice cream had hardened, we turned the basket upside down to dip the tops of the cones in chocolate. Before the chocolate dried, we dipped the tops in peanut pieces. We popped the drumsticks loose from the pins and bagged them."

—Kervin Finke (employed 1956–2006)

Pictured above: Geraldine Kincer

innate intelligence, eagerness to learn, a decided work ethic, willingness to be a team member, honesty, initiative, and an enthusiasm for life in general. Because of Ed.'s talent for employing exceptional people, his practice of providing the training and guidance needed for top job performance, and his policy of promoting from within, the key personnel he hired during the 1960s moved steadily up through the ranks to leadership roles in the company's future.

Summing Up the Sixties

The sixties proved to be a pivotal period for the company. Territory expansion into Houston and the introduction of Homemade Vanilla highlighted the era, but other events were significant. Herbert Hohlt, who had been president of the company since 1931, passed away in June 1968. The board then elected Ed. Kruse to be president; he also retained the titles of manager and treasurer. The remaining board members were Henry J. Boehm, Sr., vice president; Howard W. Kruse, assistant manager and secretary; F. C. Winkelmann, Jr.; and Sam D. W. Low.

That decade also saw the arrival of Blue Bell's Gold Rim half-gallon carton. Its distinctive appearance in the dairy case reinforced the idea of the impressive quality of the product inside the container. In a less successful venture, Blue Bell attempted to franchise two ice cream parlors in the Houston area. Despite the beauty of the stores and the quality of the products, the experiment proved unprofitable, and the two Sugar Plum stores closed within a year of opening.

The failure of the Sugar Plum stores represented merely an irregular blip on Blue Bell's radar screen of success in the sixties. In 1962 Blue Bell achieved gross sales of $1 million for the first time in its history. By the end of the decade, annual sales exceeded $4 million. The company witnessed phenomenal double-digit percentage increases in sales during each year of the decade. The 1968 sales exceeded the 1967 total by almost 30 percent. Ed. Kruse's bold decision to enter the Houston market reaped rewards that even he had never imagined.

Coconut 'n Cream

A new flavor appeared in the 1960s—as did a colorful point-of-purchase piece.

Blue Bell and Bluebonnets

Opposite page: Texas children are often photographed amid beautiful bluebonnets. Blue Bell frozen snacks certainly make posing more fun!

John Barnhill

John Barnhill's goal in life was to become a journalist and eventually own a small-town newspaper. He prepared well: He excelled academically in the Brenham public schools and earned a journalism degree at The University of Texas in 1959. After serving in the military, he began his writing career at the *Houston Press*.

His best-laid plans were thwarted, however, when Ed. Kruse enticed him to lead Blue Bell's entry into the Houston market in late 1960.

Not that John's writing skills didn't come in handy. As he knocked on the doors of Houston grocers, John developed radio spots and advertising copy for the company. He also substituted the words "Blue Bell" on cartons and in ads instead of the "B-B" in use at the time. But his greatest early contribution was his emphasis that Blue Bell Ice Cream was best, because it was made at the "Little Creamery in Brenham."

In 1969 Blue Bell employed Metzdorf Advertising to elaborate on John's theme, while John focused on expanding the company's sales territory. As Houston branch manager, then general sales manager, and eventually executive vice president of sales and marketing, John guided Blue Bell's rise to become the number-one-selling ice cream in Texas, its successful entry into the southeastern and midwestern parts of the country, and its achievement as the third-best-selling brand of ice cream in the United States.

John retired from Blue Bell in 2000. Among many other business and civic responsibilities, he currently serves on The University of Texas System Board of Regents and remains on the board of directors at Blue Bell. He and his wife, Jane (Cook), have three children—Betsy, John, and Ted—and seven grandchildren. John writes occasional columns for the *Brenham Banner-Press*.

Above: An advertisement designed and drawn by John Barnhill in the early 1960s.
Opposite page: John Barnhill paints ads on a storefront window in 1999. This photograph represents a task John performed for the company when he was still in high school.

Cookies'n Cream

Creamy vanilla ice cream with tasty chunks of chocolate crème cookies . . .
—*From an in-house description of Blue Bell's Cookies 'n Cream flavor*

A cycle of expanding sales territory followed by a need for increased and more-efficient production space was part of the Blue Bell story from the beginning. But by early 1970 the landlocked plant was bursting at the seams.

The Kruses, who had already done everything possible to increase the production capability of the plant on Creamery Street, saw no alternative. They had to construct a new facility.

Imagination Station

Where does Blue Bell get ideas for its delicious ice cream flavors? The director of research and development, Brenda Valera, cites several sources. Brenda and her assistants, Christy Moran and Leenett Jimenez, constantly monitor trends in the food industry. Employees imagine scrumptious combinations of ingredients, actually create products in their own kitchens, and send samples to any of the four plants via transport trucks. Blue Bell fans also suggest ideas. Sometimes inspiration comes from food magazines, grocery stores, dining out, children's birthday parties, reminiscences of days gone by, "what if" questions, and other even more unlikely places.

On a certain date each year, the new-flavor candidates are reviewed, and employees help to decide which ones will appear in grocers' freezers the next year. The sky's the limit in this tasty part of the ice cream industry!

Fortunately, Ed. had prepared for this eventuality. In the late sixties the company had purchased fifteen acres of property on Horton Road near U. S. Highway 290, and in early 1970 it had acquired an adjacent three and a half acres. Blue Bell would buy more acreage as it became available.

Howard had been working with architect Travis Broesche to design the new building and facilities. They presented the plans to the board and stockholders in January 1970. With official approval granted, the next several months found key personnel studying, questioning, adding, modifying, and making all the arrangements necessary to construct one of the largest and most functional ice cream plants in the nation.

Ed. had the financing lined up: earnings retained from successful years in the past; the sale of debentures to stockholders specifically for the purpose of this construction; and a $1.3 million loan commitment from a large Houston bank. With down payments made from existing funds, Blue Bell held a groundbreaking ceremony on May 26, 1971.

Ed.'s Worst Day

Ed. drove to Houston to sign the loan papers. Incredibly, when he met with the bankers, they denied the loan. Despite their earlier commitment, the loan committee had decided that the chances of a small Brenham company paying off a large construction loan by selling ice cream were slim and presented too much risk. The bankers then suggested that if Blue Bell built in Houston, the committee might be willing to revisit the issue. Ed. quashed that proposal immediately. Brenham was Blue Bell's home; it had served the company well. The bankers replied, "We don't know how to run an ice cream plant," and the discussion ended.

Ed. Kruse considers the Houston's bank's refusal the lowest point of his business career—but it didn't keep him down for long. Absolutely devastated after that meeting, he returned to Brenham determined to borrow the needed funds from local banks and savings and loans associations—but such institutions had very limited lending caps. In order to reach his goal, Ed. garnered commitments for loans at a total of five banks and savings associations in Brenham, two banks in Bellville, and one bank each in Sealy, Somerville, Burton, and Chappell Hill. Ed.'s efforts proved so successful that these accumulated offers surpassed the amount he wanted to borrow, so he now had the privilege of picking and choosing

Peanutty Paddle

A popular frozen snack in the 1970s, the Peanutty Paddle featured a large portion of vanilla ice cream encased in chocolate and peanuts.

The Long Haul

Opposite page: Mike Przyborski, who began at Blue Bell in 1966, is Blue Bell's lead transport driver. He has logged more than 4 million miles without a mishap. The Texas Safety Association named Mike the 2000–2001 Driver of the Year. In training new drivers, Mike reminds them to look ahead at the big picture and be alert to anything out of the ordinary. He also emphasizes that transports are fifty-three-foot billboards advertising Blue Bell Creameries, and poor driving habits reflect upon the entire company.

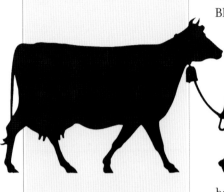

Cow and Girl Logo

In 1977 Lyle Metzdorf developed a new logo for Blue Bell Creameries—a Jersey cow being led by a little girl. Lyle felt that a "sophisticated country" image would attract attention as Blue Bell expanded its territory to Dallas and beyond.

Blue Bell Gothic

Opposite page: In the late 1970s Lyle Metzdorf used Grant Wood's *American Gothic* painting to emphasize Blue Bell's down-home approach to making ice cream. The tag line read, "Blue Bell don't taste store bought."

among willing financial institutions. For the remaining funds, the Blue Bell stockholders voted a sale of stock and restructured the earlier debenture plan.

Dreams Realized

Blue Bell finished construction and moved into the new facility in July 1972. The plant featured a 50,000-square-foot production room, a mixing room, a cold-storage warehouse, and a front office. Blue Bell invited the public to tour the plant in September of that year. In the meantime, the original facility, now designated "the Little Creamery," focused on making frozen snacks to keep up with demand. Almost as quickly as Blue Bell paid off the bank loans from its sales in ice cream, the company felt the need to increase capacity again, and in 1976 the first major expansion of the main plant began. Ironically, this time around, the Houston bank that had denied the 1971 loan eagerly financed the $2 million expansion.

Beaumont on Board

Change wasn't limited to the facilities during these years. Ed. brought John Barnhill back to Brenham to head the company's sales division in 1972 and promoted Larry Ainsworth to branch manager in Houston. As Blue Bell consolidated sales in Houston and Austin, Ed. discovered that the Carnation Company was offering its Beaumont, Texas, branch for sale. Beaumont is about 150 miles east of Brenham, very near the Louisiana border. Ed. carefully considered the problems involved with servicing customers properly at that distance from Brenham. After he had worked out the logistics and decided that Melvin Ziegenbein was the right person to head Blue Bell's third branch, the company purchased Carnation's 100 Beaumont accounts.

Howard's Worst Day

Almost before the ink had dried on the Beaumont agreement, Blue Bell faced another dark moment. A plant employee preparing to leave for home on Thursday, July 12, 1973, heard a single popping sound, smelled ammonia, and quickly alerted everyone to evacuate the cold-storage building. Anhydrous ammonia is the most effective refrigerant for large industrial facilities such as dairies and ice cream plants, but its release into the air can cause serious health problems to those exposed to its corrosive nature. In addition, the substance is flammable and explosive under certain uncontrolled conditions.

Blue Bell employees reacted instantly and properly to the crisis, but the situation remained precarious for more than thirty-six hours. Fortunately, no one was seriously injured; the ammonia was quickly shut off, and the Brenham Fire Department was on hand to provide breathing equipment for those who needed to enter the cold-storage warehouse to assess the situation. Employees took trailer loads of contaminated ice cream products to the landfill, but all personnel remained safe, and no further damage to the facilities occurred.

What made this crisis the low point of Howard Kruse's career was that it involved a brand-new, state-of-the-art facility—and discovering the cause of the problem took nearly twenty-four hours. During that time, Howard's mind whirled with worry as he considered the possibility that the entire plant might be defective. As it turned out, a line cap that had not been properly welded and annealed had blown off under pressure. Blue Bell's hardworking and dedicated personnel labored all weekend to restore the facility to normal, and thanks to their efforts, production started up as usual on Monday morning. After the cleanup, a thorough inspection revealed that all other joints and valves had been properly treated. With a thankful heart, the company moved forward.

Obstacles Overcome

The following year, Carnation closed its manufacturing plant in Houston and once again provided Blue Bell with an opportunity for growth. The creamery bought several of Carnation's accounts, as well as a sophisticated twelve-row

Jelly Terr-ible

Ed. F. Kruse was sure he had a hit. In 1976 he designed a frozen snack with a tart strawberry jelly center encased in rich vanilla ice milk with a chocolate covering. He felt that his Jelly Terror had everything a person could wish for—three desserts in one: Jell-O, vanilla ice cream, and chocolate. Ed. seemed surprised when nine out of nine salespeople vetoed the product. What did they know about the public's wishes? Determined to prove them wrong, he overrode their decision and prepared the novelty for market. It didn't sell. Ed. stated, "I thought it tasted delicious. . . . I ended up eating all of it. . . . I think I was before my time."

"MMMMMapleWalnut"
NEW ICE CREAM FLAVOR   FROM BLUEBELL

A nut with great taste.
New Vanilla Swiss Almond Ice Cream from Blue Bell

Bag a big moose.
Try our new rich Chocolate Mousse ice cream from Blue Bell.

Blue Bell tastes peachy.
Try Blue Bell's Delicious New Peaches and Vanilla Ice Cream.

Kind of nutty, but what a dish!

Blue Bell Chocolate Malt'n Fudge Nut.

Vitaline machine for making frozen snacks. Two years later, Swift and Company, where Ed. had worked before joining Blue Bell, went out of business. Blue Bell proved to be holding its own against the big ice cream players. It was no time for the company to let its guard down, however: Foremost Dairies had returned to the Houston sales area.

In 1978 the first three branches of the company were running smoothly. In fact, Blue Bell ranked number one in ice cream sales in both Houston and Beaumont and was fast approaching that status in Austin. Furthermore, the plant's capacity for production had recently increased. For those reasons, Ed. Kruse looked north toward Dallas.

Branching Out to "Big D"

Blue Bell had begun shipping frozen snacks to the Safeway stores in the area as early as 1970, and the company had

Filling Cartons by Hand

Adela Schroeder (employed 1961–1997) and Vernice Neumann (employed 1964–1997) both remember performing all steps in making ice cream and frozen snacks by hand. Even when the new plant opened in 1972, they filled cartons manually for several years. This maneuver required almost a juggling motion as an empty carton was placed under the one being filled by a stream of ice cream. The full carton was then passed to the next person for sealing, while the empty carton assumed its position under the filling nozzle. Adela, Vernice, and Lee Dell Krause (shown here) count themselves among the very few employees who perfected this motion and performed it smoothly without spillage.

performed taste tests in Dallas for two years. Ed. knew that each market had its own idiosyncrasies when it came to ice cream flavors. As the company prepared for its entry into the Dallas market, the Kroger chain, among others, expressed eagerness to sell the creamery's products.

With Dallas tastes in mind, Lyle Metzdorf developed a new logo to replace the company's long-standing bell-shaped flower. Seeking a "sophisticated country" image for Blue Bell, Lyle created a representation of a perfect Jersey cow being led by a little country girl. The innovative logo drew favorable attention immediately, especially when Lyle incorporated it into a radically different carton design that featured the cow and the girl walking completely around the lower portion of the container. The Cow and Girl logo is now the most recognizable symbol of Blue Bell Creameries.

KOOL KOOKIE™
3 Fl. Oz. Vanilla Flavored Ice Cream & 2 Oatmeal Cookies Dipped in Chocolate
Artificial Vanilla Flavor Added

The Metzdorf Agency also prepared a new media campaign for the Dallas area. It hired models dressed in milkmaid costumes to deliver half gallons of Blue Bell Ice Cream in carton-shaped Styrofoam coolers to more than 100 members of the Dallas media. This caught the attention of local newspaper reporters, radio figures, television personalities, and magazine writers, and they spread the word that Blue Bell was entering the Dallas market.

On September 18, 1978, the first day of the company's sales in the area, Blue Bell already had twenty-five accounts. By the end of its first year, the company had entered nearly two hundred additional stores and had sold almost $3 million worth of ice cream. Melvin Ziegenbein, as head of the Dallas branch, guided this success. Meanwhile, Travis Brewer, who had replaced Ziegenbein as Beaumont's branch manager in 1975, made company history by selling to the first out-of-Texas accounts, in nearby Lake Charles, Louisiana.

Back at the Plant

What else happened at Blue Bell during the 1970s? Computers appeared in the company for the first time in 1975. *The Scoop*, an in-house newspaper, began publication in 1975. Blue Bell had a booth at the Texas State Fair in Dallas in 1978. And in 1979 the company sponsored its first spring Fun Run, a ten-kilometer race, with ice cream at the finish line, to benefit Brenham High School athletics.

Fun Packaging

What else needs saying with a playful package like this?

New-Product Signage

Opposite page: These point-of-purchase pieces show a variety of Blue Bell's 1970s products, as well as Lyle Metzdorf's lighthearted way of introducing them to the public.

Cow and Girl

Following page: In 1990 artist George Hallmark painted his version of Blue Bell's Cow and Girl. He named the piece *Cream and Sugar.*

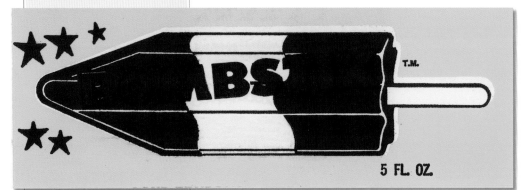

Wrap Yourself Around Blue Bell's Frozen Snacks

These treats, still produced in 2007, have had a variety of wrappers over the years. The versions shown above appeared in the early 1970s.

How the Cookies Got Into the Cream

Opposite page: Debra Westerfeld pours an open bag of Oreo cookies into a grinder for inclusion in Blue Bell's original Cookies 'n Cream Ice Cream.

Cranking It Out

As always, the most fun at Blue Bell had to do with new products. A very popular cultural phenomenon during the seventies was yogurt, appearing in every possible variation. Blue Bell's plant produced the first frozen yogurt in Texas, developing excellent low-fat and nonfat varieties. Raspberry and strawberry were the first flavors, with peach and fruit cocktail soon following. Blue Bell's frozen yogurt is noteworthy because it's made from scratch with the slow culture of live bacteria. This process protects the nutritional value of the food.

New products in the frozen snack line included Kool Kookie —a slice of ice cream sandwiched between two oatmeal

cookies and coated with chocolate. The Peanutty Paddle—a generous slab of vanilla ice cream coated with chocolate and peanuts—experienced wide popularity. The Mouseketeer— a chocolate and vanilla ice cream bar shaped like Disney's Mouseketeer face, with chocolate-coated chocolate ears— appealed especially to children.

In 1979 Blue Bell developed two of its most popular ice cream flavors. Pecan Pralines 'n Cream features praline sauce swirled into a creamy vanilla ice cream sprinkled with praline-coated pecans. Chocolate Almond Marshmallow is dark chocolate ice cream and a smooth marshmallow sauce swirled together with crisp chocolate-coated almond pieces. However, the flavor award for the decade goes to Blue Bell Cookies 'n Cream.

Cookies 'n Cream

First manufactured in three-gallon cartons in 1978, Blue Bell Cookies 'n Cream combined chunks of Oreo cookies and a creamy vanilla ice cream. Though the concept was relatively simple, the production proved extremely labor-intensive. Nabisco, which manufactured Oreo cookies, did not provide the cookies in bulk. Therefore an employee at Blue Bell actually opened each small package, as one would do at home, and placed the cookies in a grinding machine to produce the chunks, which next found their way into the vanilla ice cream.

Howard Kruse recognized immediately the potential for the success of Cookies 'n Cream, but it took more than a year before he could commit the personnel, labor, and time required for producing the flavor in half gallons for home consumption. He obviously made the right decision: Cookies 'n Cream remains the company's second all-time best seller. By the end of 1981 Blue Bell was using 1,500 cases of Oreos per week.

As the 1970s closed, Blue Bell's annual sales had reached $30 million. Employees numbered 486, and more than half of those who had worked for Blue Bell in 1951 remained on the payroll. Blue Bell now had a machine that could produce more than sixty gallons of ice cream per minute. If E. F. Kruse was flabbergasted at eighty gallons of ice cream per hour in 1937, what would he have thought about this new contraption? Could he ever have imagined that Blue Bell could produce more than ten million gallons of ice cream in 1979 alone? And what would come next?

Lyle Metzdorf

In 2002, the *New York Times* described Lyle Metzdorf as "one of the most creative people in the advertising business." Additional phrases used to portray the guiding genius behind Blue Bell's image include "funny and fun-loving," "a total perfectionist," "blessed with good taste," and "dedicated to detail."

For thirty-three years, Lyle created Blue Bell's radio spots, wrote and directed television commercials and tour films, developed ads in newspapers and magazines, and designed billboards and cartons.

Although Lyle also worked with such clients as Sony and Citibank, John Barnhill felt that Lyle most enjoyed working for Blue Bell "because he had such a rewarding part in seeing it develop from a small, country creamery to one of the nation's leading ice cream brands."

Lyle was born in 1935 in Kansas and grew up in Independence, Missouri. He attended Central College in Fayette, Missouri, and the Kansas City Art Institute and School of Design. After time in the military, he worked as a gag writer and graphic designer for Hallmark Cards in Kansas City. Lyle next went to California to be a film animator. Several advertising agencies later, he landed in Houston and opened Metzdorf Agency with his partner, Clyde Burleson, in 1965. In 1983 they sold their very successful firm to the Marschalk Company in New York, and Lyle became senior vice president and associate creative director. Later he formed Metzdorf Stone in New York, and in 1992 he returned to Houston and began Metzdorf, Inc.

Along the way, Lyle won local, national, and even international awards for his creative work, his contributions to the advertising business, and his mentoring of young talents. Lyle died in a fire aboard his sailboat, the *Matisse*, on February 18, 2002. He is survived by his wife, Martha, their children, Lance and Lisa, and several grandchildren.

Above: Lyle's 1970s hand-drawn billboard sketch. Opposite page: Lyle Metzdorf (seated) is shown with Blue Bell employees and film extras Carl Breed, Gary Stroech, and Al Novosad. They are filming "Blue Bell Remembers" for the visitors' center in August 2001.

Mint
Chocolate Chip

Refreshing, creamy mint ice cream sprinkled with delicious semisweet chocolate chips . . .
—From an in-house description of Blue Bell's Mint Chocolate Chip flavor

The booming 1980s witnessed the opening of eleven new branches by Blue Bell. The company slowly and methodically began to expand the territory it served and strengthened sales within its early branch areas.

Listing the location of the eighties branches is an efficient way to place them in Blue Bell's history, but it does not tell the story of all the sales calls made, accounts won, marketing ideas developed, ads aired, decisions made, persons involved, problems solved, media campaigns launched, hours worked, miles driven, and consumers gained.

The new branches attest to the innovation, perseverance, and no small amount of diligence that allowed Blue Bell

Our '80s Branches

Branch #5, 1980: Alvin, Texas

....

Branch #6, 1981: Fort Worth, Texas

....

Branch #7, 1982: North Dallas, Texas

....

Branch #8, 1982: Humble, Texas

....

Branch #9, 1984: San Antonio, Texas

....

Branch #10, 1985: South Dallas, Texas

....

Branch #11, 1986: East Texas (Longview)

....

Branch #12, 1986: Waco, Texas

....

Branch #13, 1988: Corpus Christi, Texas

....

Branch #14, 1989: Oklahoma City, Oklahoma
—first branch across the state line

....

Branch #15, 1989: Baton Rouge, Louisiana

Creameries to celebrate seventy-five years of business in 1982. The company thanked store owners and managers by presenting each of them with two half gallons of the flavors for 1982, Pecan Danish and Chocolate Chip Cookies 'n Cream. The company also teamed up with Continental Airlines to promote the "flight of flavors" during the last quarter of the year: Continental Airlines would deliver a cooler with two half gallons of Blue Bell Ice Cream, packed in dry ice, to any airport to which the airline flew in the United States. The cost was $19.95. More than 1,200 consumers took advantage of this offer, and the good word about Blue Bell Ice Cream flew across the nation.

Two major expansions of the Brenham facilities took place during the 1980s. Completed in 1982, the first addition doubled the production area in the main facility and made it one of the largest plants in the world. Blue Bell personnel actually completed much of the work themselves. Another enlargement, begun in 1986, increased the facility's production area still further and added cold storage and appropriate handling equipment for depositing and retrieving pallets of ice cream. Included in the second expansion were a new two-story corporate headquarters designed to reflect architectural style at the turn of the century and a visitors' center for the increasing numbers of tourists who made their way to the creamery.

Selling Scoop by Scoop

Expansion occurred on other fronts as well. Despite the failure of its Sugar Plum stores in Houston in the 1960s, Blue Bell still wanted a part of the cone-by-cone retail business. In 1985 the company developed a portable ice cream booth that could be leased to retailers. The design of these dipping stations resembled a stylized Victorian house, sported the colors of ice cream favorites, and featured the Cow and Girl logo. The portable "parlors" served seven standard flavors of Blue Bell Ice Cream and two backup flavors. Instead of the three-gallon cartons used in regular ice cream parlors, the dipping stations had special rectangular containers, each of which held six quarts of a flavor and provided for faster turnover of fresh product.

Food service manager F. C. "Sonny" Schulte did not want to compete with ice cream parlors that served milk shakes, sodas, banana splits, and other treats in addition to ice cream

Blue Bell Fun Run, 1987

This annual event has been part of the Brenham community since 1979. Proceeds benefit the athletic program at Brenham High School.

Rural Delivery

Opposite page: Blue Bell's driver salesman David Smith exchanges greetings with young consumer Coty Koehne in a 1987 photograph.

Singing for Blue Bell

Following pages: Left, Toni Price and Maryann Price prepare to sing for a Blue Bell commercial. Right, sheet music from the popular radio jingle "Blue Bell 1988."

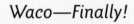

Animal Snackers.

Blue Bell Fun Shapes

Fun Shapes

These frozen desserts were animal-shaped, three-dimensional, colorful, delicious, and fun! Children in the 1980s licked them up!

Blue Bell Spreads Its Wings

Opposite page: In honor of Blue Bell's seventy-fifth anniversary, Continental Airlines offered to fly Blue Bell Ice Cream to any of its destinations. The charge was $19.95 for a cooler containing two half gallons packed in dry ice.

cones. The ice cream booths provided spur-of-the-moment sales at special events or anywhere a crowd might yearn for a cone—from malls and sporting events to hospitals, theaters, and supermarkets. Blue Bell did not manage these dip stations; the company provided the freezer cases and the ice cream to entrepreneurial individuals and retailers. The idea caught on quickly, and by the end of the 1980s hundreds of dipping stations dispensed Blue Bell Ice Cream in cones and dishes to on-the-go consumers. Among other places, Victorian ice cream booths appeared at the University of Texas M. D. Anderson Hospital and Tumor Institute in Houston, the Frank Erwin Center in Austin, and the Rand Movie Theatres in Grapevine.

Changes at the Top

Several major administrative changes took place in the 1980s, too. Ed.'s son Paul W. Kruse, an attorney in private practice who had been a member of the board of directors since 1983, joined the team at the creamery as legal counsel in 1986. Diana Markwardt, who had joined the company in 1969, became Blue Bell's first woman vice president as she took charge of office operations. Bill Rankin joined the company as administrative assistant to Ed. in 1981, then saw his responsibilities steadily increase until he became chief financial officer and treasurer. Ed. Kruse, still in the top leadership position, assumed a more efficient four-day work schedule in 1986. He remained Blue Bell's chief executive officer and chairman of the board, while Howard Kruse advanced from assistant general manager to president.

Devoted to promoting talent from within its ranks, Blue Bell had always emphasized excellent job-specific training programs for its employees. In 1986 Howard created Blue Bell University and established the company's first ice cream manufacturing course for key personnel. It was modeled after the ice cream course at Penn State University. One night each week for a year, the students met to examine topics in dairy science, ice cream production, refrigeration, quality control, nutrition, and plant safety. To round out their education, the participants learned Blue Bell's history and thoroughly studied its sales program. Experts from various areas of the company acted as instructors, assigning students homework and administering exams, calculating grade point averages,

and determining class rankings. Over the years this manufacturing course, even in its shortened nine-month term, has produced thoroughly educated management teams throughout the company.

Another 1980s initiative was the Supreme Suggestion program. This plan encouraged plant employees to contribute ideas for making operations "easier, faster, less costly and safer through procedure changes, equipment modifications, energy conservation and safety improvement." The annual winners are presented with Udder Best Awards, but the operations process reaps the true rewards.

New Approach to Advertising

The innovative Blue Bell Advertising Associates arrived in Brenham in 1987. Lyle Metzdorf and Clyde Burleson, owners of the Metzdorf Advertising Agency when Blue Bell signed on in 1969, had long since sold their successful firm. At various times, the men had joined other agencies and moved to different cities. Although Blue Bell had stayed with the two advertising geniuses every step of the way, the constant change of photographers, artists, media contacts, and designers interfered with continuity in the ad program. For that reason, Blue Bell brought virtually all of its advertising activities

Waco—Finally!

In 1980 a billboard appeared in Waco: "Dear Blue Bell: Can't Get Your Ice Cream in Waco. Help!" Wacoans were perplexed. Blue Bell had been available in Austin, ninety miles to the south, since 1965. In 1978 Blue Bell had opened its first Dallas branch, ninety miles to the north. When the Waco branch finally opened in 1986, the formerly bypassed residents breathed a welcome sigh of relief!

This holiday season, Blue Bell ice cream is really taking off.

Because in celebration of our 75th anniversary, Blue Bell is flying just about anywhere Continental Airlines flies the Proud Bird Express.*

That gives you over 70 destinations to choose from. So you can fly Blue Bell ice cream to your friends in New York City, Chicago or dozens of other cities. And send their taste buds soaring.

To take advantage of this heavenly new departure, simply fill out the coupon and mail to the little creamery in Brenham.

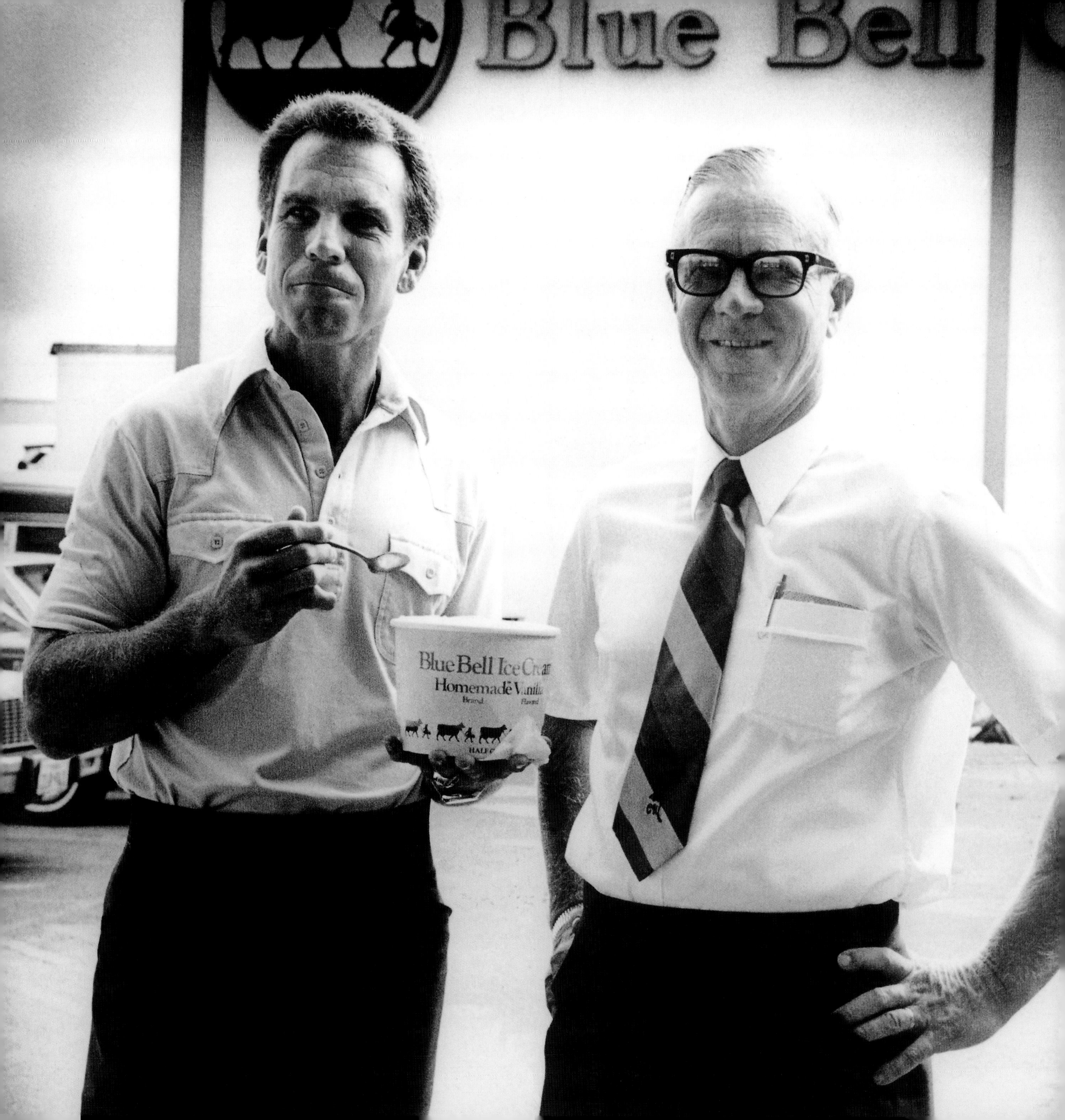
Blue Bell
Blue Bell Ice
Homemade

Famous Visitors

Earl Campbell, running back for the Texas Longhorns, the Houston Oilers, and the New Orleans Saints and NFL Hall of Famer

....

President George Herbert Walker Bush

....

President George W. Bush

....

Nolan Ryan, pitcher for the Mets, Angels, Astros, and Rangers and Baseball Hall of Famer

....

Lloyd Bentsen, U.S. senator and secretary of the treasury

....

"Mean" Joe Greene of the Pittsburgh Steelers and NFL Hall of Famer

....

U.S. Senator Kay Bailey Hutchison

....

Roger Staubach, Dallas Cowboys quarterback and NFL Hall of Famer

....

Kenan Thompson, actor, star of Nickelodeon's *Kenan & Kel*

....

Jennifer Berry, Miss America 2006

in-house and hired its own personnel to do daily tasks. It then retained Lyle and Clyde as creative and media/marketing consultants, respectively.

The new arrangement proved advantageous for all concerned. The ever-innovative Lyle developed two new films for the Blue Bell visitors' tour, and his television advertisement about needing more Blue Bell frozen snacks in Needmore, Texas, earned a regional Telly award. And continuing Blue Bell's tradition of winning prestigious awards for its advertising and marketing, the pastoral setting featured on a Blue Bell package of frozen snacks even won a Clio, one of the advertising industry's highest recognitions.

Successful Innovations

What products were Lyle's clever ads promoting in the 1980s? Many new flavors were introduced, among them Blueberry Cheesecake, Caramel Turtle Fudge, Nutty Coconut, and Peanut Brittle. Rainbow joined the sherbet products, and several new Country Custard flavors were unveiled. Newfangled frozen snacks included Pudding on a Stick, Cherry Slush Squeeze-Ups, and fun, three-dimensional novelties like Monsters.

Other changes came in response to consumers' requests for products using NutraSweet. In addition to lighter versions of Bullets and Fudge Bars, in 1989 the company introduced Diet Blue Bell. Calories were substantially reduced in this frozen dessert by substituting NutraSweet for sugar and halving the butterfat of Blue Bell's original ice cream. The new product came in several flavors: Vanilla, Dutch Chocolate, Neapolitan, Strawberries 'n Cream, Pineapples 'n Cream, and Peaches 'n Cream. The company became the first in the nation to sell diet products in half-gallon cartons.

In the same year, Blue Bell instituted one of its most successful charity events when Pint-for-a-Pint blood drives began in the Houston area. Offering a pint of Blue Bell Ice Cream to people who donated a pint of blood brought attention to this life-giving cause. The idea spread throughout Blue Bell sales territory and continues as an important part of the company's annual contribution to its communities.

Blue Bell ended the 1980s with a 60 percent market share in Houston, Dallas/Fort Worth, and San Antonio. The 1990s seemed equally promising: In 1988 Blue Bell had purchased twenty acres of land in Broken Arrow, Oklahoma, and at the close of the decade the company was designing its first major plant outside the state of Texas.

No Sugar Added

This product was called Diet Blue Bell in the 1980s. Substituting NutraSweet for sugar, Blue Bell offered a delicious low-calorie product for those watching their waistlines.

Roger Staubach

Opposite page: The legendary Dallas Cowboys quarterback visited Blue Bell Creameries in 1988. Here he chats with Ed. Kruse and enjoys some Homemade Vanilla Ice Cream.

Howard W. Kruse

Howard William Kruse was born on August 1, 1930, in Brenham, Texas, to E. F. and Bertha (Quebe) Kruse. He received his education in the Brenham Independent School District, where he was an honor student and an athlete, lettering in football, basketball, and track at Brenham High School.

After graduating in 1948, he attended Texas A&M University in College Station, Texas. There he served in the Corps of Cadets and was selected as a regimental commander. He graduated in 1952 with a B.S. in dairy manufacturing and earned the honor of distinguished student for his 2.93 GPA on a scale of 3.0. Immediately after graduation, he became a lieutenant in the U.S. Army in the Korean War.

Having worked part-time for Blue Bell Creameries during his youth, Howard joined the company on a full-time basis in 1954. He was named assistant manager in 1956 and directed plant operations from that point forward. In 1986 he was named president of Blue Bell, and then president and chief executive officer in 1993. He officially retired from Blue Bell Creameries on April 30, 2004, but he remains president emeritus of the company and continues as a director.

Howard has served as president of the Brenham Rotary Club, the Washington County Chamber of Commerce, the Dairy Products Institute of Texas, St. Paul's Evangelical Lutheran Church of Brenham, and the Washington County United Way Fund. He is a past commander of the American Legion Buddy Wright Post #48, former scoutmaster of Troop 742, past secretary of Bohne Memorial Hospital, and a former Sunday school teacher at St. Paul's Evangelical Lutheran Church. His community honored him as Washington County Man of the Year in 1990.

Howard was inducted into the Texas Business Hall of Fame in 1993. In 1995 he was named Lutheran of the Year by Lutheran Social Services of the South. He was inducted into the Dairy Products Institute of Texas Hall of Fame in 2000. Two years later he was selected as a Distinguished Alumnus by Texas A&M University and received the Ruby McSwain Outstanding Philanthropist Award from the National Agricultural Alumni and Development Association. He was inducted into the Texas A&M Corps of Cadets Hall of Honor in 2003, and with his brother, Ed., he received the Ernst and Young Entrepreneur of the Year Award in 2005.

Currently, Howard serves on the board of trustees of Scott and White Memorial Hospital and the Scott, Sherwood, and Brindley Foundation in Temple. He chairs the Campaign Leadership Committee of the Texas A&M Agriculture Program for the "One Spirit One Vision" Campaign. He is an advisor for the Texas A&M Health Science Center and a director for the Southern Association of Dairy Food Manufacturers.

Howard Kruse is married to the former Verlin Kautz. They have four children, Diane, Kathryn, David, and Jim. The Kruses currently have seven grandchildren.

Driver Salesman
A Day in the Life

O nce Blue Bell employees have manufactured their delicious products and eaten all they can, the driver salesman has the privilege of delivering ice cream and frozen snacks to the rest of the consumers. His most important duty is to make sure that Blue Bell's products avoid "heat shock" and arrive in perfect condition for each customer's enjoyment.

The workday of a driver salesman often begins as early as 2:00 a.m., because he wants to have plenty of fresh products, attractively arranged in clean freezer cases, when the shoppers arrive. A typical daily route might include grocery store chains, major discount stores, convenience stores, drugstores, schools, and hospitals. Among other locations for delivery are sports complexes, restaurants, theme parks, hotels, office buildings, and university campuses. Often a driver salesman, the distinctive public face of the company, feels like a celebrity on his route because consumers ask him questions about favorite flavors or exclaim, "There goes the Blue Bell man!"

Opposite page: This scene is from Blue Bell's television commercial "First Day," which humorously depicts a driver salesman's initial day at the company.

These storyboards, hand drawn by Lyle Metzdorf, eventually became Blue Bell's 1995 "First Day" television commercial. Despite the serious mission of the driver salesman to deliver Blue Bell products in prime condition, unexpected incidents sometimes occur. Nevertheless, he always arrives at his destination with delicious Blue Bell Ice Cream and frozen snacks —at least, those he hasn't eaten along the way!

DATE: **11 MAY 1993**

CLIENT: **BLUE BELL CREAMERIES**

PRODUCT: **NEW MARKETS**

JOB NUMBER: **BB-93106**

LENGTH: **:30 SECONDS**

TITLE: **"SLOW DELIVERY"**

VIDEO

AUDIO:

Open on young man saying goodbye to his mother.

BB truck driver: **Bye mom.**
Mom: **Be careful, you've never been to a city.**

ANNCR (VO): SOME TIME AGO, A YOUNG MAN LEFT

(MUSIC THROUGHOUT)

Cut to young man (eating ice cream) driving old truck out of town past Brenham city limits sign.

ON AN IMPORTANT TRIP TO DELIVER A SPECIAL ICE CREAM MADE IN BRENHAM, TEXAS...

Cut to young man driving old truck along beautiful country road (eating ice cream) with barn in background.

(Blue Bell ice cream carton painted on barn.)

IN THE OLD FASHIONED WAY TO TASTE HOMEMADE.

THROUGH THE YEARS...

Cut to young man (eating ice cream) driving old truck across stream.

BLUE BELL HAS BECOME TEXAS' MOST POPULAR ICE CREAM...

Cut to young man (eating ice cream) in old truck–stopped while mama pig and babies cross road.

(Could be chickens, ducks, cows, dogs, cats or any other cute animal to show country local.)

SOME SAY, "IT'S THE BEST IN THE COUNTRY".

METZDORF, INC.
1730 NASA ROAD ONE, SUITE 101
HOUSTON, TEXAS 77058, USA
713.333.0444, FAX 333.0304

TELEVISION

DATE: **11 MAY 1993**
CLIENT: **BLUE BELL CREAMERIES**
PRODUCT: **NEW MARKETS**

JOB NUMBER: **BB-93106**
LENGTH: **30 SECONDS**
TITLE: **"SLOW DELIVERY"**

VIDEO:

Cut to old truck with flat tire as young man nonchalantly eats ice cream.

AUDIO:

Anncr:(VO): CONSIDERING WE STARTED IN 1907...

Cut to old truck with radiator boiling over while young man eats another bowl of ice cream.

Anncr:(VO): YOU MIGHT SAY IT TOOK US A LONG TIME TO DELIVER BLUE BELL TO YOUR STORE...

Cut to young man and grocer standing next to old truck.

Grocer: **What took you so long?**

Truck driver: **Sorry, sir.**

Grocer: **Well, unload it.**

Young man opens back of truck to reveal one lonely half gallon of Blue Bell homemade vanilla left.

Grocer: **Where's the rest of my order?**

Truck driver: **I ate it all.**

Cut to close up of lone half gallon in back of truck.

Anncr:(VO): BLUE BELL, WE EAT ALL WE CAN AND WE SELL THE REST.

Super: **Now in Kansas City**

METZDORF, INC.
1730 NASA ROAD ONE
SUITE 101
HOUSTON, TEXAS 77058, USA
713.333.0444, FAX 713.333.0304

Through the years Blue Bell's driver salesmen have indeed encountered challenging situations. There have been floods, hurricanes, ice storms, tornadoes, and Texas "blue northers." Driver salesmen have happened upon the scene of robberies, inmate escapes, and hostage-taking events. Their routes have been interrupted by traffic jams and opportunities to aid stranded motorists. Nothing, however, keeps them from the "swift completion of their appointed rounds"!

Rainbow
Freeze

A rainbow on a stick!
The frozen confection is layered with tasty flavors of grape, lime, lemon, orange, and cherry . . .
—From an in-house description of Blue Bell's Rainbow Freeze frozen snack

With fifteen branches all up and running, and another eighteen scheduled to open in the 1990s, Blue Bell needed to make more ice cream. Despite twenty-one major expansions since 1972, the company could have added yet more production space in Brenham, but management decided that the new plant should be closer to areas where sales were expanding.

North Texas was proving to be a vigorous market for Blue Bell's products, and the company already serviced routes in Oklahoma and beyond. These territories meant long jaunts for transport drivers traveling from Brenham to the distribution branches. Therefore Ed. and Howard decided to build a manufacturing facility north of the Little Creamery.

O . . . klahoma

They chose Broken Arrow, on the outskirts of Tulsa, for several reasons: proximity to the expanding territory, family-friendly quality of life, suitable land, community enthusiasm for the project, and availability of industrial revenue bonds for financing the plant.

Solving a Mystery

On April 17, 1991, a young woman appeared on the South Rim of the Grand Canyon with no memory of who she was, where she was from, or how she had traveled to Arizona. After talking to the woman for some time, the sheriff gleaned only three bits of information: The woman mentioned Delchamps, a grocery store chain in the southeastern part of the United States; she referred to a river; and she repeated the slogan "Blue Bell, the best ice cream in the country." The sheriff called the creamery to see if the company could help solve the puzzle. Knowing that Blue Bell serviced Delchamps in the eastern part of Texas as well as the western portion of Louisiana—and that the Sabine River lay between the two states—the spokesperson for the company suggested that the authorities focus on that area of the country. Television stations in eastern Texas and western Louisiana showed clips of the woman. Her parents saw the video, contacted the sheriff, and brought her home safely.

Acting as consultants to the architects and engineers, Howard Kruse and Eugene Supak, who managed Blue Bell's plant operations, dived into the design process for the 100,000-square-foot facility. Construction began in 1991 and continued through 1992, with the first products being manufactured on October 13, 1992. Blue Bell invited the city of Broken Arrow to the plant's grand opening in May 1993. Despite stormy weather and the need to shelter some two thousand people in the plant's basement for a short period of time, more than nine thousand people attended during the two-day celebration. The visitors enjoyed tours of the manufacturing facility and, of course, free Blue Bell Ice Cream. By the end of 1993 the plant had produced more than five million gallons of ice cream and employed more than 100 people.

Sweet Home Alabama

With much growth in the southeastern portion of the United States, Howard Kruse became extremely interested in an ice cream plant for sale in Sylacauga, Alabama, a small rural community southeast of Birmingham. In 1996 the Land O' Sun Dairy of Johnson, Tennessee, had closed its Flav-O-Rich ice cream production facility in Sylacauga and had laid off most of the 136 workers until a new owner could be found. Pete Moore, the former operations manager of the plant, called Paul Kruse and asked if Blue Bell would be interested in purchasing the facility.

Once again Howard Kruse and Eugene Supak joined forces to study the situation. Because of the company's unique way of organizing production lines and its high procedural standards, Blue Bell had never before considered buying an existing facility. However, after visiting Sylacauga, carefully surveying the plant's production capabilities, being assured that needed adjacent property was available for purchase, meeting with former employees, and discussing the situation with the city leadership, Howard decided to proceed with the purchase. He also gained the confidence of the laid-off workers as he began hiring them to help with the extensive renovations of the plant.

Blue Bell's fourth manufacturing facility, with more than 100,000 square feet of space, began operations in May

Last year we ran an advertisement, stating that people outside of Texas couldn't get Blue Bell Ice Cream.

But this year we're making an exception because President George Bush calls Texas his home.

So during his term as President, we'll be sending Mr. Bush his favorite Blue Bell Ice Cream flavors.

It's the little creamery's way of saying, "Congratulations, Mr. President."

Blue Bell Goes to Washington

When George Herbert Walker Bush entered the White House as the forty-first president of the United States in 1989, Blue Bell temporarily expanded its territory to include that one location in Washington, D.C.

Meet Belle

Opposite page: Belle is the famous Jersey cow who stars and sings in many Blue Bell commercials. Although her public schedule takes her to various locations for photographic sessions, special charity events, and Blue Bell functions, Belle much prefers her serene life at home in the Jersey Barnyard in La Grange, Texas. There she stands around in her pasture eating lots of grass, alfalfa hay, and grain mixture, rests under her shade tree, and receives much attention from the Frerichs family, who own her. Belle also enjoys listening to classical music while producing more than two thousand gallons of milk each year.

To MY BLUE BELL FRIENDS — WITH BEST WISHES !

Love at First Bite

In 1995, the astronauts on the space shuttle *Atlantis* needed to transport a small freezer to the space station, so they filled it with Blue Bell Mini-Sandwiches and Blue Bell Homemade Vanilla and Cookies 'n Cream ice cream cups. The cosmonauts aboard the Russian space station Mir thought the treats were out of this world!

The Good Ol' Days

Opposite page: In a scene from Blue Bell's 1995 television commercial "Country Day," siblings are transported back to simpler times of their youth.

1997. At the public grand opening in April 1998, Jon Searles, the manager of the Sylacauga plant, greeted the visitors and informed them that the new plant currently employed 130 people, only 3 of whom were from Brenham. He hinted at plans for expanding the plant in the future and adding even more workers. The town leaders of Sylacauga expressed delight in the renovations and the boost to the community's economy.

International Opportunities

As it turned out, the market for Blue Bell was growing globally as well. The 1990s witnessed spirited interest in international sales. The ice cream and frozen snacks that the four Blue Bell plants manufactured were not solely for consumption in Texas, the Midwest, the South, or elsewhere in the United States. The company's first trailer load of product for Mexico left Brenham in August 1990. The Tinajero brothers introduced Blue Bell products through their Paletas Manhattan retail stores in Guadalajara, Puerto Vallarta, Manzanillo, and Colima.

All this is not to say, however, that love for Blue Bell was restricted to the North American continent. In late 1991 Blue Bell sent a container of Homemade Vanilla cups to Japan for trial distribution through the Fujisan Company of Japan. Other foreign countries that have received containers of Blue Bell products since the early 1990s include Greece, the United Arab Emirates, Saudi Arabia, Oman, and Kuwait.

With the world's appetite for Blue Bell growing, by the end of the century only constant plant expansions, additions, and manufacturing innovations made it possible to fill the company's 770 trucks and deliver Blue Bell products to 581 wholesale routes. To that end, during the 1990s, the company increased the size of the kitchen and fruit-processing areas, improved its research and development laboratory, introduced in-plant forming of half-gallon cartons, built a three-story addition for increased office space, storage, and meeting purposes, installed cone-baking units, and added hardening systems.

Among updates at the Little Creamery was an expansion that allowed wrapping machines to be attached to the Vitalines, which manufactured frozen snacks. The Broken Arrow and Sylacauga plants had no sooner held their public openings than Howard designed plans for their extensions and improvements. Some of the branches required additional cold storage, office space, receiving bays, or parking areas. Throughout the 100-year history of the company, plant and equipment improvements have been an integral part of the Blue Bell story.

Outer Space and Cyberspace

Highlights of the 1990s moved beyond making, selling, and delivering ice cream when, in 1995, Blue Bell saw its products heading for outer space as NASA astronauts took a little Texas hospitality with them to the space station Mir.

Our '90s Branches

Branch #16, 1990: Tulsa, Oklahoma

Branch #17, 1990: West Texas (Big Spring)

Branch #18, 1991: New Orleans, Louisiana

Branch #19, 1991: Rio Grande Valley (Harlingen, Texas)

Branch #20, 1992: Ruston, Louisiana

Branch #21, 1993: Kansas City, Kansas

Branch #22, 1994: Mobile, Alabama

Branch #23, 1995: Jackson, Mississippi

Branch #24, 1995: Montgomery, Alabama

Branch #25, 1995: Birmingham, Alabama

Branch #26, 1997: Little Rock, Arkansas

Branch #27, 1997: Huntsville, Alabama

Branch #28, 1997: New Braunfels, Texas

Branch #29, 1998: Atlanta (East), Georgia

Branch #30, 1998: Atlanta (West), Georgia

Branch #31, 1998: North Texas (Lewisville)

Branch #32, 1998: Memphis, Tennessee

Branch #33, 1999: Lafayette, Louisiana

Dear Blue Bell

This is Howard Kruse's favorite letter, and it affected him so deeply that he reinstated the manufacture of Fruit Special Ice Cream.

I am, at the present time, residing as an inmate in the Texas Dept. of Corrections. Life here isn't as hard as many are led to believe, although it does get lonely at times; for the most part prison makes a person stronger and healthier. Here one learns to deal with life and all its many faces; for example, when my father died I managed to take it like a man; I faced the hurt and sorrow. My wife divorced me a few months ago, obtaining custody of my daughter in the process. Once again I was able to face what lay before me. Then my wife sold our home, all my tools, gave the dog away and ran off with a close friend, driving my new four wheel drive truck, which they wrecked. I do not have insurance on the truck. I realize that this is my problem not yours but I merely wish to show you the extremes to which a man can suffer and still recover with some resemblance of pride.

Last week something devastating happened that has left me rattled. The officer who works the unit commissary told me that you no longer make Fruit Special Ice Cream. Why? How could you take a man's only means of pleasure in a place like this; it's cruel. Do you know; can you even imagine how many evenings I've spent lost in the delights of a pint of Fruit Special? I guess not! I admit that your other flavors are quite delicious, but this one in particular was my favorite of all time! I just don't know how to take this news. What happened?

I'm sure that in time I'll get over all this, but until I do I'll live in sadness eating Homemade Vanilla, Cookies and Cream and the rest. Take care and I hope to hear from you soon.

Sincerely,
H.L.
Richmond, Texas

P.S. My mother told me my dog came back.

After Blue Bell's foray into outer space, could the Internet be far behind? In 1998 the company launched its Web site, www.bluebell.com. The site offered a variety of information to Web surfers: Blue Bell history, availability of ice cream flavors and snacks, answers to frequently asked questions, description of the processes for making ice cream, directions to the creamery for tours, helpful telephone numbers, and how to order a cooler of ice cream for someone unfortunate enough to live in an area outside Blue Bell's sales territory.

Back to Basics

While enlightening its consumers through cyberspace, Blue Bell addressed education in a broader and more traditional manner. In 1999 it began rewarding Teacher of the Year finalists and nationally recognized Blue Ribbon School winners with ice cream parties. That practice continues today.

In the meantime, several of Blue Bell's enduring ice cream flavors appeared for the first time and quickly became part of its year-round roster of flavors: Chocolate Chip Cookie Dough, Strawberries & Homemade Vanilla, and Banana Split. Blue Bell also developed Homemade Vanilla Light, a delicious boon for weight watchers. The Rainbow Freeze proved to be one of the company's most popular products. Consumers loved this colorful item, as they did Blue Bell's complete line of mini-snacks and the new Country Cone frozen snacks. Three super-premium bars also appeared in the 1990s: Homemade Vanilla, Double Fudge, and Almond. Sometimes in with the new also meant out with the old. In 1991 Blue Bell removed mellorine from its list of products; the vegetable-oil-based frozen dessert had been in the line for forty years.

Howard Rises to the Top

The creation of new plants, branches, expansions, flavors, and other activities took place during a period of transition for Blue Bell Creameries. In 1993 Ed. Kruse reduced his work week by half and relinquished his role as chief executive officer to Howard Kruse, who assumed day-by-day management of the company. Ed. remained chairman of the board.

In a similar action later in the decade, John Barnhill decreased his week to four days but continued as executive vice president of sales and marketing. He turned over the position of general sales manager to Melvin Ziegenbein.

Despite all the changes, by the end of 1999 Blue Bell ranked as the number three branded ice cream in the country while being available in only twelve states. Furthermore, the company announced to its employees and stockholders that it was Y2K compliant and ready to welcome the new millennium.

New Carton

Banana Split Ice Cream appeared for the first time in the 1990s. Its carton was also new, with larger images of the Cow and Girl displayed.

Kids and Snacks

Opposite page: Blue Bell's frozen snack packaging in the 1990s featured adorable children, along with delicious treats.

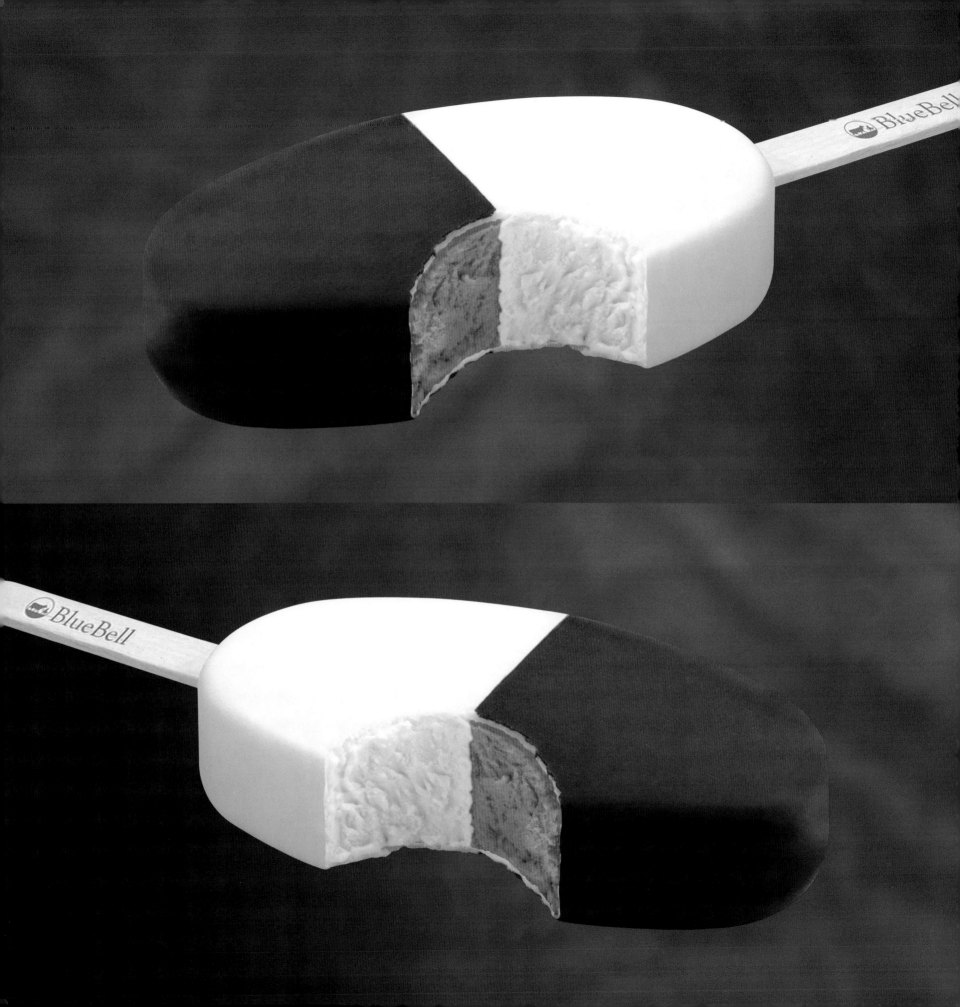

Great
Divide Bar

A vanilla and chocolate frozen treat dipped in a vanilla coating, then half dipped in a rich chocolate coating . . .

—From an in-house description of Blue Bell's Great Divide Bar

A s the great divide between the 1900s and the 2000s disappeared smoothly across Asia, computers continued to function and the Y2K doomsayers' predictions proved wrong. That calamity averted, the new millennium was still fresh when the events of September 11, 2001, occurred.

Blue Bell employees responded from afar with blood drives and fundraisers. Contributions of free ice cream to many nonprofit organizations also helped generate funds to aid the victims and their families.

Closer to home, the company experienced challenges in its expanded territory. Four hurricanes hit Florida in 2004; the eye of Hurricane Katrina passed directly over Blue Bell's New Orleans branch in 2005; and less than a month later

Millennium Branches

Branch #34, 2000: Atlanta (South), Georgia
....
Branch #35, 2001: Jacksonville, Florida
....
Branch #36, 2002: Lufkin, Texas
....
Branch #37, 2002: Tallahassee, Florida
....
Branch #38, 2003: Orlando, Florida
....
Branch #39, 2003: Tampa, Florida
....
Branch #40, 2004: El Paso, Texas
....
Branch #41, 2004: Charlotte, North Carolina
....
Branch #42, 2005: Phoenix, Arizona
....
Branch #43, 2005: Nashville, Tennessee
....
Branch #44, 2006: Columbia, South Carolina
....
Branch #45, 2006: Katy, Texas

Hurricane Rita pounded the Beaumont, Texas, area. With generators and refrigerated trucks, Blue Bell's tireless personnel were in a unique position to deliver ice and to otherwise come to the assistance of those affected in Florida, Louisiana, Mississippi, Alabama, and Texas.

Addressing Different Tastes

Having its sales territory spread over many states certainly exposed Blue Bell to increased weather-related events, but opportunities abounded and far outweighed the risks. As the company's branches moved farther and farther from Brenham, the concept of creating regional flavors developed. Determining that Central Texas did not have a monopoly on taste buds, Blue Bell introduced Key Lime Pie Ice Cream to its consumers in Florida. The flavor proved so popular that Blue Bell decided to offer that little bit of Florida to the rest of its sales regions and make it a rotational flavor for the entire company. Other favorite regional flavors included Mardi Gras Ice Cream, offered in the Gulf Coast regions where pre-Lenten celebrations take place early each year, and Mississippi Mud Pie Ice Cream in the Mississippi Delta area, including parts of Tennessee, Mississippi, Arkansas, and Louisiana. Heart of America Ice Cream appeared in Kansas City, Cantaloupe 'n Cream became an August treat in Texas, and Georgia Peach Cobbler Ice Cream found popularity in that state.

The welcome acceptance of regional flavors inspired the creation of southwest flavors, especially those for consumers south of the border and along the southwestern border with Mexico. Dos Amigos added a hint of cinnamon to the unique flavoring of Mexican vanilla swirled with a Mexican chocolate ice cream. The Tres Leches con Fresas flavor featured delicious pieces of "three milks" cake and sweetened strawberries in a rich, creamy vanilla ice cream. Other ice creams in the southwest line included Dulce de Leche and Buñuelos.

A more traditional flavor, Wedding Cake Ice Cream, attracted much attention in 2004 as betrothed couples competed in contests that awarded gallons of the delectable dessert to be served at their weddings. This bride's cake delicacy featured pineapple ice cream blended with crushed pineapple, walnuts, vanilla wafers, and shredded coconut and swirled throughout with cream cheese icing. Chocolate Covered Strawberries, introduced in May 2006, offered a possible groom's component to the wedding theme.

Meeting Consumers' Needs

Always invested in promoting good health, Blue Bell had its nutritionists working very hard to develop products appro-

Blue Bell Barn

Through the years there have been many renditions of a barn featuring Blue Bell Ice Cream advertising. This watercolor from the 1990s is by Kitty Keller.

Holiday Cheer

Opposite page: Blue Bell's corporate headquarters is ready for the holiday season, a sure sign to devoted fans that Peppermint Ice Cream has returned to their grocer's freezer case.

A Natural Teacher

Howard Kruse enjoys explaining the ins and outs of making Blue Bell Ice Cream to a group of schoolchildren.

The Best Part of Our Tour

Opposite page: Eric Bridges enjoys a cup of his favorite flavor of Blue Bell Ice Cream following a 2006 tour of the plant in Brenham.

priate for consumption at schools. Although ice cream had been part of the school lunch program since the 1940s, state officials, concerned with growing numbers of overweight youngsters at the turn of the twenty-first century, created new guidelines for items sold to schoolchildren. Blue Bell quickly satisfied the strict requirements of those statutes with smaller individual-portion ice cream containers and additional vitamin-enriched frozen treats.

Across the country, the portability of single-serving frozen snacks became increasingly popular among adults on the go. Blue Bell created special freezer cabinets for use in convenience stores, thus allowing easier access to ice cream for hungry consumers in a hurry. New products like the Great Divide Bar, the Megabite, and the Chocolate Éclair Bar joined enduring standards like the Country Cone, the Chocolate Chip Country Cookie, the Double Fudge Bar, the Nutzo Cone, and many others.

Changing of the Guard

The creation of new flavors, product lines, branches, and programs took place as Blue Bell faced major staff changes. In 2000 John Barnhill retired from the company. He had steered Blue Bell's sales, advertising, and marketing since 1960, and although he remains on the board of directors, his valuable daily contributions to the company ended with his retirement. In 2002 Lyle Metzdorf died tragically in a boating accident. The death of the creative genius behind Blue Bell's image, radio and television ads, and media campaigns left a tremendous void in the company. In May 2003 Howard Kruse

announced that he would retire the following year. He promised to continue developing flavors and advising in any way possible. He became president emeritus in May 2004, his fiftieth year as a full-time worker at the company.

Blue Bell, a company with long-standing success and excellent personnel, weathered these difficult losses and continued on its way. Melvin Ziegenbein stepped into John's shoes as vice president of sales and marketing, while Ricky Dickson became general sales manager. Clyde Burleson, Jim Hayhurst, Carl Breed, and a host of talented people who had worked with Lyle combined their strengths to keep his ideas and visions for the company alive. Eugene Supak was firmly ensconced in the management of plant operations. Paul Kruse, secretary and legal counsel for Blue Bell, accepted the reins from Howard and became chief executive officer and president.

As Blue Bell Creameries approached its centennial year, it employed nearly 3,000 people, had 45 branches, serviced almost 900 wholesale routes in all or parts of sixteen states, owned a fleet of 1,500 trucks, and produced 267 different products yearly. The company also welcomed the changing of its street name in Brenham from Horton Street to Blue Bell Road.

After 100 years of growth, new products and big successes, one might wonder how Blue Bell can continue to refer to itself as the "Little Creamery in Brenham." The company never hesitates to state the truth: Despite the transformations of the past 100 years, Blue Bell remains a small-town company with small-town values. That fact will never change.

Photo courtesy Richard Korczynski, Victoria, Texas

Home, Sweet Home

In June 2004 Jim Boyd, AFCAP Ranger with the United States Air Force, found a card buried in the sand at Camp Taji, Iraq. Addressed to "Timothy," the card featured a photo of a pint container of Blue Bell Homemade Vanilla Ice Cream filled with bluebonnets and the Lone Star flag in the background. Inside the card, a handwritten note declared, "Wish we could send you a case of cool ice cream. Don't think it'll make the trip. Take care and we look forward to your return. Love Robert and Donna."

Jim Boyd placed the card near his bunk. "It is hard to put into words the way I felt when I found this postcard from my great home state of Texas. It was lying on the ground in an area totally destroyed by our bombs. . . . Each time I looked at the card I was reminded of home and Texas and what it would be like to go to the food store in Austin and buy some Blue Bell Ice Cream. . . . I had mixed feelings of being happy and homesick at the same time, but mostly happy."

Birthday Cake

Vanilla ice cream with pieces of chocolate cake, a chocolate icing swirl, and bright multicolored sprinkles . . .
—From an in-house description of Blue Bell's Birthday Cake flavor

Many celebrations and commemorations are planned for Blue Bell Creameries' 100th anniversary. A sculpture garden is being established in the grassy area in front of the visitors' center in Brenham.

Bronze statues of E. F. Kruse, Ed. F. Kruse, and Howard W. Kruse will stand in one area, providing a thoughtful counterpoint to the bronze statue of the iconic Jersey cow and little country girl in the other portion of the garden.

Artistic Contributions

Veryl Goodnight is creating the Cow and Girl sculpture, while Robert Hogan is crafting the Kruse figures. Table-size replicas of the Cow and Girl sculpture will be showcased in the Little Creamery, Broken Arrow, and Sylacauga plants. The Texas Historical Commission has awarded a historical marker to Blue Bell Creameries, and that tablet will be part of the sculpture garden as well.

Blue Bell has also commissioned a special painting to commemorate its first 100 years. Created by artist Benjamin Knox, the original canvas will reside in Brenham, and copies will be placed in the other three production facilities and in all of the branches.

Branch Celebrations

A special centennial tractor-trailer will travel to all the Blue Bell sales territories with an exhibit titled "Blue Bell: 100 Years." The trailer has been designed to fold open on one side, and the interior will have displays featuring Blue Bell's history, products, and manufacturing processes. While the trailer is in each sales territory, that branch will hold its centennial celebration with customers and consumers. Needless to say, plenty of free Blue Bell Ice Cream will be available for all those attending the events. A smaller trailer will sell Blue Bell merchandise and show favorite Blue Bell commercials. In each community, Blue Bell will host the local Boys and Girls Clubs for a special sneak preview of the exhibit and will contribute sales proceeds to their worthy programs.

Festivities in Brenham

In Brenham, Blue Bell will also sponsor several activities. One celebration will honor the company's employees, present and past. Another will focus on saluting customers, suppliers, and vendors. An additional celebration is slated to recognize the stockholders, many of whom are Blue Bell employees.

The main event in Brenham will be a three-day public celebration at the Washington County Fairgrounds, July 19–21, 2007. At this "Day in the Country" festival, ice cream lovers from all over Central Texas will enjoy free Blue Bell products, the trailer exhibit, cow-milking demonstrations, local entertainment, and other centennial activities. In Broken Arrow, Oklahoma, the annual "Taste of Summer" celebration will expand to include the trailer exhibit and other entertaining events focusing on Blue Bell's 100 years in business. A similar event is planned for Sylacauga, Alabama.

Widespread Enjoyment

Consumers and fans who are unable to join in the actual festivities will nevertheless be able to participate. Special flavors of ice cream and innovative frozen snacks marking the centennial year will appear in grocers' freezer cases, and a unique centennial version of the Cow and Girl logo will adorn Blue Bell packaging and advertisements during 2007. In addition, creative juices will flow as ice cream lovers compete in the "Name the Flavor" contest, which will launch in January 2007. Details and rules will appear at www.bluebell.com.

Perpetual Pleasure

While all the celebrating takes place, Blue Bell will proceed with business as usual: the production of superior ice cream and frozen snacks, the establishment of new sales territories, and the improvement of plant facilities. And we will continue to make plans for 2008 and beyond.

As always, at the top of our list is the pledge to bring smiles to our valued consumers as they enjoy the best ice cream in the country!

Homemade Vanilla Cup

What birthday party would be complete without cups of Homemade Vanilla and wooden spoons? Blue Bell also makes cups of Dutch Chocolate and Birthday Cake.

Centennial Logo

At left: During the centennial celebration of 2007, Blue Bell's Cow and Girl logo will be enhanced to represent Blue Bell's first 100 years.

A Family Affair

Opposite page: Howard Kruse, Ed. Kruse, and Paul Kruse continue the Blue Bell legacy handed down to them by their father and grandfather E. F. Kruse.

BLUE BELL
100
YEARS
1907 - 2007

Paul W. Kruse

Paul William Kruse was born to Ed. F. and Evelyn (Tiaden) Kruse on October 7, 1954. He attended schools in the Brenham Independent School District and graduated from Brenham High School as salutatorian. Paul received a B.B.A. in accounting from Texas A&M in 1977.

In 1980 Paul earned a law degree at the Baylor University School of Law, where he made the Baylor Law Review and served as president of the law students' association.

After graduation Paul engaged in the private practice of law in Brenham. He was elected to the board of directors of Blue Bell Creameries in 1983. In 1986 he gave up his law practice to work full-time at Blue Bell as legal counsel. In that same year he was named corporate secretary, and in 1991 he was named a vice president of the company. Upon Howard's retirement in 2004, Paul was elected chief executive officer and president.

He has been chairman of the Trinity Medical Center, the Blinn College Foundation, and the Dairy Products Institute of Texas and is a member and past president of the Brenham Rotary Club.

He served as chairman of the International Ice Cream Association from 2003 to 2005, and received the Soaring Eagle Award from the International Dairy Foods Association in 2006.

Paul is married to the former Barbara McMartin. They have three children: Audra, Wes, and Gwen. They belong to St. Paul's Evangelical Lutheran Church of Brenham. Paul enjoys hunting and engages in farming and ranching as time permits.

Extra Toppings

Anecdotes, letters, facts, and photos like these add to the fun of making Blue Bell Ice Cream!

Dear Blue Bell

Unfair Hiring Practices

I'm writing this letter as a formal complaint against the corporation and its management regarding the hiring practices at Blue Bell Creameries!

I have searched for Pistachio Almond ice cream for months and months, but to no avail. Thus, I've come to the conclusion that the management of Blue Bell has maliciously conspired to hire only those employees whose favorite ice cream is Pistachio Almond.

I know that the only reason I can ever find my favorite ice cream is that one of your employees is out sick, on vacation, or on some sort of special assignment. Therefore, I strongly urge the management of Blue Bell to change the current hiring practices to include individuals who display or develop a strong tendency towards (or desire for) other flavors; so maybe, just maybe, a trickle of Pistachio Almond will leak out to those of us who eat "the best ice cream in the country."

Sincerely,

D.B.
Carrollton, Texas

"Alamo a la mode"

Crayola has a crayon to represent each of the fifty United States. The Texas Crayola is named "Alamo a la mode" in honor of the Alamo in San Antonio and Blue Bell Creameries in Brenham.

A Strange Request

Paul W. Kruse received a call from the director of the Star of the Republic Museum at the nearby Washington-on-the-Brazos State Historical Park. The museum possessed a stuffed buffalo that had developed an insect infestation. A researcher at the museum had discovered that freezing the buffalo for a certain period of time would kill the bugs, permitting the display to defrost would allow any eggs to hatch, and subsequently placing the animal back under freezing conditions for a while longer would settle the problem. Could Blue Bell help?

Blue Bell had assisted several museums after hurricanes and floods by allowing their sodden materials to be preserved under freezing conditions, but this was a most unusual request. Paul contacted the transportation department to see if it had an old refrigerated truck that could be used in this situation. With an affirmative answer, Blue Bell resolved the museum's buffalo problem.

Fireworks for Sale!

In the '50s and '60s, Blue Bell sold fireworks during the Christmas and New Year's holidays. Ice cream sold slowly during the winter months, so the cherry bombs, sparklers, Roman candles, and other colorful displays bolstered the company's bottom line.

Blue Bell product display at the State Fair in Dallas in the mid-1970s.

"Blue Bell, for the uninitiated, is the best ice cream in Texas, which, naturally, makes it the best ice cream on earth."

—*Sports Illustrated*, May 9, 1989

Dear Blue Bell

Can't Get Enough

I'm not the type of person to write letters unless totally necessary. This letter is totally necessary. I had seen your commercials so the name was somewhat familiar. When I passed the display in the freezer section I said I'll try a pint. I started my car and opened my Blue Bell Buttered Pecan so I could eat it on the way home. After one spoon, I took my car out of reverse and put it back in park. After two spoons, I turned off my engine. When I reached the bottom of the carton I had no choice but to leave my groceries, go back inside the store and purchase 2 more big containers. This ice cream was so creamy and sweet and the pecans so fresh and crunchy, it's like the cashier added the nuts before she rang me up!

This is hands down the best ice cream I've ever eaten. I just wanted to say thank you for sharing Blue Bell with Orlando. I don't know if I should be glad it's finally available here or mad because it JUST became available here!

Keep up the good work!

D.E.
Orlando, Florida

Doug Middleton Goes Bananas

Blue Bell makes a conscious effort to recycle as many items as possible. One such endeavor involves banana peels, which are a by-product of delicious treats like Banana Pudding Ice Cream and Fudge Bombstiks.

Doug Middleton, manager of the ingredients processing department, took the time to transport each day's banana peels to a piece of property where he'd bury them in a compost heap. One day he was in a hurry and just dumped the peels—intending to bury them the next day. However, when he returned, all the banana peels were gone. The same set of events occurred the following day. On the third day, when Doug drove up to the compost site, thirty cows came running to his truck. The cows loved eating the banana peels!

Blue Bell now has a chute that goes directly from the banana-peeling station to a truck that delivers banana peels to Brenham farmers for their delighted cows.

Jennifer Berry, Miss America 2006, is a devoted fan of Blue Bell Ice Cream. On one of her countrywide tours, she traveled to Brenham to visit Blue Bell Creameries.

Dear Blue Bell

Rising Creek

One morning our aunt frantically called to let us know the creek was rising and was about to get in her house. She got out, the water got in . . . 12 inches.

That afternoon, my husband waded in to try to save any items of value before they were ruined by mud and water. We waited for the silver and jewelry, ready to clean them up. He came back with four half-gallon cartons of Blue Bell Ice Cream and a cherry pie.

This just shows what lengths my husband will go to for Blue Bell.

J.W.
Burkeville, Texas

Taste Testers

Any employee at Blue Bell can become a taste tester. Panels are used to sample and evaluate ice cream flavors and frozen snacks. More-sophisticated palates become important when fresh dairy products arrive from the farms. Only the best milk and cream are unloaded at Blue Bell. Lab technicians perform the dairy taste tests, and they also sample mixes before they enter the processing stage. These experts easily distinguish between Milk Chocolate mix and Dutch Chocolate mix, Homemade Vanilla mix and French Vanilla mix. At specified points during the manufacturing process, the lab personnel sample the ice cream to assure its quality, and the finished products receive one last test before they are packaged and delivered to customers. The taste testers want to make sure that each carton of Buttered Pecan, Cookies 'n Cream, Strawberries & Homemade Vanilla, and every other flavor meets Blue Bell's high standards of excellence in every respect.

Mailing Blue Bell

1. Get a Styrofoam cooler.

2. Place crinkled newspaper in the bottom of the cooler.

3. Place five pounds of dry ice in a two-inch block form on top of the newspaper. (Dry ice pellets could be used instead.)

4. Place more crinkled newspaper on top of the dry ice.

5. Nest cartons of ice cream together in the cooler.

6. Fill empty spaces with more crinkled newspaper.

7. Place lid on cooler.

8. Seal cooler lid to base with freezer tape.

9. Pack ice chest in cardboard packing box, seal, and address.

10. Ship by FedEx or Airborne Express for next-day delivery.

11. Inform the recipient so he can be present when the package arrives.

12. Better yet, let Blue Bell do it! www.bluebell.com.

Cadillac Ranch

The playful side of Lyle Metzdorf is demonstrated in his computer-generated version of Stanley Marsh 3's *Cadillac Ranch* sculpture in West Texas.

Rural Good Recipes

In 1984 Blue Bell held a recipe contest in seven Texas cities to discover the most delicious dessert using Blue Bell Ice Cream as the main ingredient. Twelve hundred people submitted recipes. Kathryn Minyard of Garland, Texas, received the grand prize, a trip to Maui, for her Blue Bell Pecan Delight Pie. Second place, a half gallon of Blue Bell Ice Cream each week for a year, went to Helen Chambers of Houston, for her Lemon Candy Ice Cream Pie. Blue Bell published a recipe book containing the top fifty recipes.

Blue Bell Pecan Delight Pie

Kathryn Minyard, Garland, Texas

Ingredient list:

3 egg whites

1 cup sugar

1/2 teaspoon vanilla

1 cup crushed pecan shortbread cookies or buttery-flavored snack crackers

1/2 teaspoon cinnamon

1/2 cup chopped pecans

1 quart Blue Bell Pecan Pralines 'n Cream Ice Cream, softened

1 small jar caramel topping

Whipped cream

Instructions:

Preheat oven to 350 degrees.

Beat egg whites until stiff. Gradually add sugar and continue beating until egg whites are glossy and form stiff peaks. Add vanilla.

Mix crushed cookies (or crackers), pecans, and cinnamon. Fold cookie mixture into beaten egg whites.

Pour into well-greased 10-inch pie plate. Smooth out center and build up sides to form shell.

Bake for 30 minutes at 350 degrees.

Cool completely before adding filling.

Soften ice cream just enough to stir. Fill cooled shell with ice cream. Spread caramel topping over ice cream, reserving about 2 tablespoons for final garnish.

Place in freezer for 1 hour. Top with whipped cream and drizzle with reserved caramel topping.

Lemon Candy Ice Cream Pie

Helen Chambers, Houston, Texas

Ingredient list:

One 9- or 10-inch graham cracker piecrust

1 tablespoon graham cracker crumbs, reserved

3 quarts Blue Bell Homemade Vanilla Ice Cream

1 cup (1/2 lb.) lemon sour balls, crushed fine

1/8 teaspoon yellow food coloring

Instructions:

Prepare graham cracker crust, reserving 1 tablespoon graham cracker crumbs for topping. Place crust in freezer until ready to fill.

Let 1 1/2 quarts of the ice cream soften slightly; keep the reserve quarts in the freezer.

Crush lemon sour balls fine in blender.

Turn softened ice cream into medium bowl and add crushed candy and food coloring. Stir with wooden spoon just until mixture is combined and ice cream is evenly colored.

Spoon ice cream mixture into crust and freeze, covered with foil, until firm, about 6 hours.

Remove reserved 1 1/2 quarts Homemade Vanilla from freezer. Top pie with round scoops of ice cream.

Sprinkle reserved graham cracker crumbs on pie.

Cover and return to freezer.

Take out of freezer about 10 minutes before serving time. (The pie keeps well in the freezer.)

Punch Clock

For a long time, creamery workers documented their time at work with this punch clock. Made by the Simplex Time Recorder Company, the clock used rubber bands, thumbscrews, and brass gears to keep consistent records of employees' hours.

Traffic Jam

East Texas driver salesman Eddie Post found himself caught in a nightmarish traffic jam along I-20 east of Longview. Making the best of a bad situation, Eddie passed out Fudge Bombstiks to the stranded motorists. Needless to say, tensions eased a bit.

Blue Bell's Coming to Phoenix!

Regional manager Harold Gilson traveled to Phoenix, Arizona, in 2005 to assist in opening the territory. Searching for a store in Scottsdale, Harold and the driver salesman found themselves at a dead end on a tiny road. As they endeavored to discover their location on a map, a woman slammed on her brakes behind them, jumped out of her Jeep, ran to the Blue Bell truck, and exclaimed, "Are y'all really coming to Phoenix?!" Receiving an affirmative answer, she yelled back to her daughter in the Jeep, "Yeah, they're really coming!" She further screamed, "We're so happy!" And, back to the Jeep, "Aren't we, honey?!" The woman's conversation with the Blue Bell people and her daughter in the Jeep lasted several more exchanges. Finally, Harold discerned that Buttered Pecan was the woman's favorite flavor, so he offered her a half gallon. As the Blue Bell truck turned back up the road, the woman and her daughter remained in their car happily eating Buttered Pecan. That sort of excitement is priceless!

Dear Blue Bell

Secret Recipe

We have always been Blue Bell fans, especially since what I am about to tell you happened.

Our church was having an ice cream supper and when I make "homemade" ice cream, I always have to have my husband "do" the ice cream freezer.

On this particular Saturday, my husband and I were having a "heated" disagreement, and I wasn't about to ask him for help.

Without saying anything to my husband, I went to the store and purchased two half gallons of Blue Bell Homemade Vanilla and brought it home.

While my husband sat at the kitchen table, I proceeded to wash out the ice cream freezer, dip my Blue Bell into the container, pack it, put the lid on, pour the ice around the container, put ice cream ice on top, and a towel over the top of that. My husband never said a word—he is a very intelligent man!

At the supper, I'd guess there were 30 different freezers of ice cream and when a friend tasted mine, he began to rave about how great it was. The line shifted quickly to our ice cream freezer and soon it was gone, while others had ice cream to take home.

Everyone wanted to know my recipe. I didn't tell until the next day at church when one man mentioned my "wonderful" ice cream. I finally told them, but I've regretted it ever since—the next month was our chili supper and no one trusted me. But many have used my "Blue Bell" recipe since.

Thank you,

D.C.
Rockwall, Texas

2006 Top 10 Flavors

Homemade Vanilla

....

Cookies 'n Cream

....

Dutch Chocolate

....

The Great Divide

....

Strawberries & Homemade Vanilla

....

Buttered Pecan

....

Natural Vanilla Bean

....

Banana Split

....

Moo-llennium Crunch

....

Chocolate Chip Cookie Dough

Saved by the (Blue) Bell

One never knows what problem Blue Bell will solve. In an episode of television's popular series *Murder, She Wrote*, Chocolate Decadence Ice Cream inadvertently saved a woman's life. She had eaten the treat before accidentally ingesting poison. The ice cream coated her stomach, slowed the absorption of the poison, and kept her alive until she received the needed antidote!

Frozen Snacks Circa WWII

Salesman Andy Anderson would return from a road trip late at night during the war years. Upon his arrival, he, Mrs. Anderson, E. F. Kruse, Mrs. Kruse, and E.F.'s daughters, Bertha and Mildred, would go to the creamery and make frozen snacks until they had enough products for Andy's route the next morning.

Our Flavor Fiascos

Not all of Blue Bell's flavors have been instant hits. Some were ahead of their time . . .

Jelly Terror
A frozen snack with a tart strawberry jelly center encased in rich vanilla ice milk and coated with chocolate

....

Dill Pickle 'n Cream
Green ice cream with small pickle chips

....

Licorice
Ice cream that turned consumers' mouths black

....

Purple Fink Bar
A raspberry ice cream product that left the consumer's mouth purple

....

Macadamia
A nutty ice cream that just never caught on

....

Peanut Butter
Another nutty ice cream that maybe needed jelly

Texas Task Force 1 Search and Rescue Team members appear with Paul Kruse after returning from Ground Zero in 2001. Blue Bell Creameries managed to send ice cream to the team during its mission following the World Trade Center terrorist attacks of September 11.

Schlitterbahn Ice Cream Coke Float

An exciting ice cream event occurred on July 12, 1986: Blue Bell teamed with Coca-Cola to create the world's largest Coke float. With 1,500 gallons of Blue Bell Vanilla Ice Cream and 2,800 gallons of Coca-Cola, the Coke float made quite a splash at the Schlitterbahn Water Park in New Braunfels, Texas, where it was concocted. The 13,100,100-calorie event, which benefited the Leukemia Society of San Antonio, earned a place in the *Guinness Book of World Records*. The 27-foot "glass" from the Coke float later became the anchor of the soda straw slides at the theme park.

Lacy Sodolak, one of Blue Bell's Country Girls, enjoys introducing Blue Bell Ice Cream to new markets. This photo was snapped for an article in the *Gaston (N.C.) Gazette* on October 13, 2004.

Blue Bell's Star Power

Race car driver A. J. Foyt received gift certificates for 287 gallons of Blue Bell Ice Cream from Chevrolet upon his retirement in 1991.

—*Brenham Banner-Press*, August 30, 1991

Comedian Bob Hope loved Blue Bell Ice Cream, so friend, professional golfer, and fellow Blue Bell fan Doug Sanders, kept Hope's freezer filled with frequent shipments from Texas.

—*Houston Post*, May 30, 1982

Sarah Ferguson, former British royalty and spokesperson for Weight Watchers, treated herself to berries topped with Blue Bell Ice Cream as a dessert following a light meal.

—*Houston Chronicle*, October 12, 2004

These women are enjoying Blue Bell Mini Sandwiches on a Continental Airlines flight in 1990.

Dallas Cowboys running back Emmitt Smith prepares for a Super Bowl XXX victory in 1996 by enjoying some Blue Bell ice cream.

Dear Blue Bell

Miracle Cure

Our nine-year-old miniature schnauzer suffered a very traumatic accident. My husband was hanging a swing on a 4x4 timber when it came tumbling down on her head. After rushing her to our vet, we found she had a concussion and a smashed nose. We watched her for hours into the night. She refused both food and water.

About midnight, my husband went to the freezer for his usual late-night snack (Blue Bell, of course!) and brought it into the bedroom where we had the dog. She raised those little ears and added what sparkle she could to those swollen eyes and acted as though she wanted some, too. She licked the spoon with all the strength she could muster and with each bite got stronger. After finishing off the whole dish, she stood up . . . something she hadn't done in eight hours! This was definitely a turning point!

She still has a while to recover and will probably be blind in one eye, but thank you Blue Bell for getting her on the road to recovery. You saved the day with your great product that not just people love!

Sincerely,

K.A.
Pineland, Texas

"Resolve the next time you are in Texas to obtain the best ice cream in the world, which is made by Blue Bell Creameries of Washington County."

—*Time* magazine, August 10, 1983

The Territories of Blue Bell

From our initial tiny sales territory in Brenham, Texas, Blue Bell now markets ice cream in parts or all of sixteen states. Because of Blue Bell's policy of personally delivering our products to your grocer's freezer, we have depended upon our branches to expand our territory.

A branch is a local sales office and distribution center. Tractor-trailers transport Blue Bell Ice Cream and frozen snacks from a plant to the branch. At the branch's loading dock, shipping clerks unload the products into a sophisticated cold-storage area with a temperature of -18° Fahrenheit. The products remain in cold storage until driver salesmen, in their bobtail trucks, deliver them to local stores and other sales locations. Additional sales personnel include the branch manager, the sales manager, territory managers, and route supervisors. They all maintain office space in the branch but spend most of their day out on sales calls. Office personnel support the selling and distribution operations.

The following map shows where Blue Bell's branches and territories have spread over the past 100 years.

Opposite page: Without the Broken Arrow and Sylacauga plants, Blue Bell's distribution would be limited. The Sylacauga plant (shown here) services many of the branches in the southeastern portion of the United States.

Blue Bell Territories

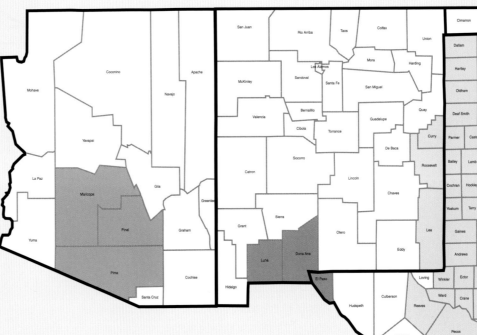

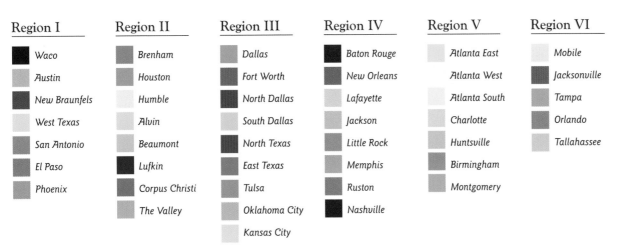

Key to Regions

Region I
- Waco
- Austin
- New Braunfels
- West Texas
- San Antonio
- El Paso
- Phoenix

Region II
- Brenham
- Houston
- Humble
- Alvin
- Beaumont
- Lufkin
- Corpus Christi
- The Valley

Region III
- Dallas
- Fort Worth
- North Dallas
- South Dallas
- North Texas
- East Texas
- Tulsa
- Oklahoma City
- Kansas City

Region IV
- Baton Rouge
- New Orleans
- Lafayette
- Jackson
- Little Rock
- Memphis
- Ruston
- Nashville

Region V
- Atlanta East
- Atlanta West
- Atlanta South
- Charlotte
- Huntsville
- Birmingham
- Montgomery

Region VI
- Mobile
- Jacksonville
- Tampa
- Orlando
- Tallahassee

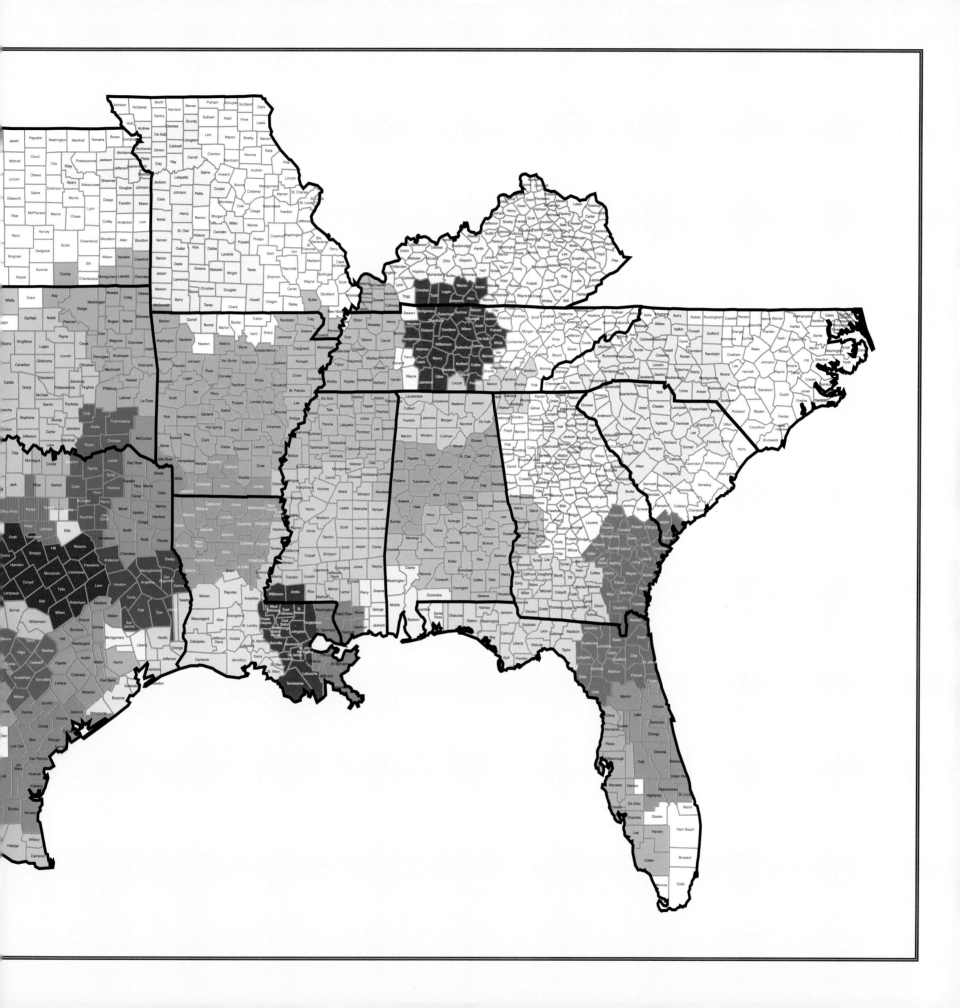

ACKNOWLEDGMENTS

"It's a cinch by the inch but hard by the yard."

—ED. F. KRUSE, BLUE BELL CREAMERIES, BRENHAM, TEXAS

Producing Blue Bell Ice Cream requires the best people, ingredients,
and processes available. Conceptualizing, researching, writing, designing,
and publishing this history of Blue Bell demanded the same level of
expertise and commitment from many devoted people. The following groups
deserve recognition and thanks for their contributions to this book.

Cream of the Crop
ED. F. KRUSE AND HOWARD W. KRUSE
Without their entrepreneurial vision and total dedication, which led to Blue Bell's success, there would be no story to tell. Without their interviews and permission to access historical documents, the story would be incomplete.

Production Supervisor
PAUL W. KRUSE
He envisioned the book and provided the moving force behind it with his time, enthusiasm, and total support.

Production Line
JENNY ANDERSON, CARL BREED, JIM HAYHURST, BILL WEISS
This crew from Blue Bell devoted many hours to researching facts, providing visuals, writing, proofreading, verifying details, and attending meetings.

Cherry on Top!
RUTH GOEKE
She put the finishing touches on every aspect of the book—just as she does with everything else Blue Bell produces.

Flavor Creator
DERRIT DEROUEN
He was the creative genius who designed the layout and brought the book to life.

Quality Control
BARBARA RODRIGUEZ
She edited the manuscript and, according to another slogan at Blue Bell, did what few others can do: She made a silk purse out of a sow's ear.

Mix Processing
MISSY COLBERT, PROJECT MANAGER
KAY BANNING, BRIAN BIRZER, KRIS BRUINSSLOT, AMBER BYFIELD, CAROLYN CHAVANA, KATIE COUGHLIN, FRANK CURRY, MARYBETH DAIGLE, DAVID BARR DUNHAM, LOUISE FLAIG, SYLVIA GRIEGO, MICHAEL LEVY, REBECCA MACDONALD, SARA MCCABE, JAN MCINROY, ROSE RANKIN, SHANNON STAHL, MARY PAT WALDRON, ROB WALLACE AT THE WHITLEY COMPANY
These talented, hardworking, and patient wonders at Texas Monthly Custom Publishing added the necessary expertise, compassion, and humor to keep the project on track and on time and make it a reality.

Factory Tour
GREG BRIDGES, JASON JENKINS, KELLY MARKOS, DOUG MIDDLETON, CHRISTY MORAN, DALE SOMMERLATTE, BRENDA VALERA, WAYNE WINKELMANN
They willingly opened their departments at Blue Bell to countless and time-consuming questions concerning processes and procedures.

Driver Salesman
JIMMY CULP
He graciously and patiently shared a day in his life as a driver salesman in Austin, Texas.

Basic Ingredients
AGNES "ANDY" ANDERSON, JOHN BARNHILL, JR., HERBERT "BUCK" BENDER, ROBERT BORCHGARDT, RICKY DICKSON, KERVIN FINKE, LARRY GIBBS, JOHN GILLESPIE, HAROLD GILSON, GILBERT GOEKE, JR., HERBERT GOESSLER, DAVE HELLMANN, WAYNE HUGO, STEVE JAMES, CLARENCE JASTER, ELWOOD JASTER, LEEROY KRAMER, EUGENE LEHMANN, JAMES LIEPKE, HERMAN "BUTCH" LORENZ, DIANA MARKWARDT, CLARENCE MATHIS, WILBERT "BUDDY" MEIER, VERNICE NEUMANN, LIONEL NEWSOME, AL NOVOSAD, MARK PATRANELLA, MIKE PRZYBORSKI, WILLIE SCHNEIDER, ADELA SCHROEDER, DARRELL SCHULTE, KATIE SCOTT, EUGENE SUPAK, BILLY RAY WINKELMANN, MELVIN ZIEGENBEIN, JR.
They contributed their memorable stories of Blue Bell Creameries—together, their years at Blue Bell exceed a millennium.

Special Flavors
PEGGY CAMPBELL, SUE CHANDLER, COURTNEY COUFAL, CHERRYL DURRENBERGER, RITA GASKAMP, ERICH GLENEWINKEL, GREG JOHNSON, CAROL KOEHNE, KIM ORSAK, KELLI REMMERT, BARBARA SAUNDERS, DOTTIE SCHAER, SARA SCHRAMM, PHYLLIS WEISS
They responded to each request for help and information enthusiastically, accurately, and efficiently.

Visitors to the Creamery
DONNA BRIDGES, ERIC BRIDGES, GREG BRIDGES, MADISON BRIDGES, PEGGY CAMPBELL, THOMAS CAMPBELL, SUE CHANDLER, RACHELLE ETZEL, JARRETT HALFMANN, LINDSEY HALFMANN, RUSSELL HALFMANN, JODIE HENSKE, BRIAN HORAK, BRIANNA HORAK, WENDY HORAK, JASON JENKINS, LISA JENKINS, SAMUEL JENKINS, ZACHARY JENKINS, SCOTT MEADOWS, CHERYL MIDDLETON, DOUG MIDDLETON, LAUREN MIDDLETON, RYAN MIDDLETON, BRITTANY TIADEN
These Blue Bell family members donated their time and talent to help with photographs for the centennial book.

Jerseys
TED BARNHILL, FLOYD JENKINS, *Scoop* EDITORS AND CORRESPONDENTS
Their articles and videos over the years provided a treasure trove of Blue Bell learning and lore.

Green, Green Grass of Brenham
BEST WESTERN HOTEL, *BRENHAM BANNER-PRESS*, BRENHAM HERITAGE MUSEUM—ESPECIALLY DR. WILFRED DIETRICH, CORA BENNETT, CORENE NIEMEYER, CONSTANTIN BARBU, JOANNE DOHERTY, AND CLARENCE HODDE, DR. W. F. "BOY" HASSKARL, JR., GLORIA NIX, PATRICIA PIAZZA, RED ROOM RESTAURANT, NANCY CAROL ROBERTS MEMORIAL LIBRARY—ESPECIALLY JENNY UR
These mainstays of Brenham supplied essential information, sustenance, and rest.

Mix-Ins
ANN ANDERSON, AIDA BARRERA, THE GALVESTON GIRLS, HERBERT AND LETHA HOHLT, THE MACINERNEY FAMILY—ESPECIALLY ED, ED, JR., DOUG, ERIC, MERRIE, KIM, KAREN, DYLAN, GILLIAN, ERIN, CONNOR, CULLEN, ABBY, AND IAN, THERESA MAY, THE MCLEOD FAMILY, KATHLEEN RICE, WILLIAM WARREN ROGERS, ALICE WYGNANT
Their personal touches and professional guidance gave valuable support to this production.

Ice Cream Lovers
Blue Bell's sincerest thanks go to every person who has ever eaten, bought, sold, recommended, provided ingredients for, or advertised our products. Your delight in our ice cream and frozen snacks will continue to be our highest priority.

Index

Italic page numbers refer to illustrations.